WALDORF EDUCATION
AND ANTHROPOSOPHY

2

[**XIV**]

FOUNDATIONS OF WALDORF EDUCATION

RUDOLF STEINER

Waldorf Education and Anthroposophy

2

Twelve Public Lectures

NOVEMBER 19,1922 – AUGUST 30,1924

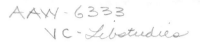 Anthroposophic Press

*The publisher wishes to acknowledge the inspiration
and support of Connie and Robert Dulaney*

❖ ❖ ❖

Introduction © René Querido 1996
Text © Anthroposophic Press 1996

The first two lectures of this edition are translated by Nancy Parsons Whittaker and Robert F. Lathe from *Geistige Zusammenhänge in der Gestaltung des Menschlichen Organismus,* vol. 218 of the Complete Works of Rudolf Steiner, published by Rudolf Steiner Verlag, Dornach, Switzerland, 1976. The ten remaining lectures are a translation by Roland Everett of *Anthroposophische Menschenkunde und Pädagogik,* vol. 304a of the Complete Works of Rudolf Steiner, published by Rudolf Steiner Verlag, Dornach, Switzerland, 1979.

Published by Anthroposophic Press
RR 4, Box 94 A-1, Hudson, N.Y. 12534

Library of Congress Cataloging-in-Publication Data

Steiner, Rudolf, 1861–1925.
 [Anthroposophische Menschenkunde und Pädagogik. English]
 Waldorf education and anthroposophy 2 : twelve public lectures.
November 19, 1922–August 30, 1924 / Rudolf Steiner.
   p. cm. — (Foundations of Waldorf education ;14)
 Includes bibliographical references and index.
 ISBN 0-88010-388-4 (pbk.)
 1. Waldorf method of education. 2. Anthroposophy. I. Title.
II. Series.
LB1029.W34S7213 1996   96-2364
371.3'9—dc20   CIP

10 9 8 7 6 5 4 3 2 1

Printed in the United States of America

Contents

WITHDRAWN

Introduction

The present collection of public lectures given by Rudolf Steiner between 1922–1924 has not previously appeared in English. It may be regarded as a continuation of the collection of public lectures printed under the title *Waldorf Education and Anthroposophy 1*.

By this time Rudolf Steiner had achieved considerable public prominence. His lectures and travels were regularly reported in the press, and the Waldorf school movement was gaining increasing recognition. Emil Molt, the owner and managing director of the Waldorf Astoria Cigarette Factory and a longtime anthroposophist, had made this educational movement possible by asking Steiner to found a school at his factory. At its inception, the school provided a broad education for the children of the workers. Emil Molt was conscious of the needs of the working people; his social commitment was generous and profound.

From that endeavor arose the first Waldorf school, which opened its doors in Stuttgart in September 1919 with one hundred and thirty children in eight grades. After four years, it had grown to accommodate eight hundred students in twelve grades. By then, many families outside the Waldorf Astoria factory had enrolled their children in this progressive enterprise, directed by Rudolf Steiner himself.

Rudolf Steiner's various trips to the Netherlands, where he also spoke publicly about Waldorf education, led on Palm Sunday, April 9, 1922, to the birth of an initiative for the founding of the first Waldorf school in Holland. The courses on education that Rudolf Steiner gave in England at Oxford (1922), Ilkley, Yorkshire (1923), and Torquay, Devonshire (1924) led to the founding of the first Waldorf school in the English-speaking world. This occurred early in 1925, still during Rudolf Steiner's lifetime, and the school is now known as Michael Hall, in Forest Row, Sussex. Today the Waldorf movement comprises more than six hundred schools worldwide. Some one hundred and fifty are located on the North American continent. In 1928 the first school in America opened its doors in Manhattan, New York.

These public lectures emphasized the cosmopolitan nature of an education that recognizes the human being as consisting of body, soul, and spirit. It is significant that in Holland, a country known for its openness to the world, Rudolf Steiner spoke about the necessity of a global Waldorf movement, which in fact was achieved some thirty-five years later.

Between 1919 and 1924, Rudolf Steiner gave some two hundred and seventy lectures on education. They can roughly be divided into five categories:

1. Lectures held exclusively for the first teachers of the Waldorf School in Stuttgart. These largely consisted of a training course and included seventy conferences with the growing faculty of the school.
2. Courses on education given to teachers, and sometimes the public at large, in Switzerland, England, Holland, and Germany between 1920 and 1924.
3. Public lectures, such as the ones contained in *Waldorf Education and Anthroposophy 1* and in the present volume.
4. A scanty number of written works, consisting of a small collection of articles and an early basic booklet, entitled, *The Education of the Child in the Light of*

Anthroposophy. At first sight, it may seem surprising that Rudolf Steiner did not write a basic manual on Waldorf education such as one might find in the works of Piaget, Skinner, and others. There is no conceivable reason why he could not have produced such a work when, between 1919 and 1924, he wrote a number of books on other subjects. It is important to realize that he favored the dissemination of the new Waldorf ideas on education by word of mouth rather than through the printed medium. To learn to understand this art of education, it is preferable to do so by way of dialogue and practical examples.

5. In the fullness of Rudolf Steiner's lectures on non-pedagogical topics, an astonishing number of longer (and sometimes shorter) references can be found with regard to the education of children, often with special warnings that unless pedagogical methods are changed, future generations would be much harmed in their development. To date, these passages have not been assembled in one volume.

Two basic considerations are taken up in March 1923 in Stuttgart: What is the relationship of pedagogy and art, and what is the relationship of pedagogy and the moral life? These lectures were held in a vast hall, attended by large audiences. Rudolf Steiner also addressed the assembled public when he introduced a eurythmy performance by the students of the Stuttgart Waldorf School, which was now celebrating its fourth year. Here, he emphasized that eurythmy forms an inherent part of the curriculum for all children, and described its nature as an ensouled form of gymnastics.

On June 30 and July 1, 1923, he spoke publicly in Dornach about Waldorf education. The lectures could no longer take place in the Goetheanum building, a wooden structure of great beauty that had been totally destroyed by fire on New Year's Eve, 1922/1923. In reading what Rudolf Steiner said in 1923, a particularly difficult year in the history of the anthroposophical movement, one would hardly be aware of the immense loss suffered, not only by Rudolf Steiner, but also by many others. Instead of dwelling on the tragedy, Rudolf Steiner worked during that year with untiring enthusiasm and produced a model for the second Goetheanum, which was to occupy the same site as the wooden building and which stands to this day.

The lecture of July 1 offers a totally new perspective not found anywhere else in his lectures. Rudolf Steiner discusses the fact that unless the child, approximately between the ages of seven and fourteen, is introduced in a living way to the Christ along the lines of an education out of anthroposophy, the youngster will either deny the Christ or will hold on to a traditional faith by means of which he or she cannot truly experience the Resurrected One.

Steiner stresses the importance of founding an educational art on two pillars. On the one hand must be an ethical approach and on the other an insight into the true soul nature of the child.

In the companion volume, mention was made of Rudolf Steiner's visit to England in 1922 and the invitation he received to lecture in April, in Stratford-on-Avon.

In fact, one of his main presentations was given on the "real Shakespeare day," April 23, St. George's Day, which is commonly regarded both as Shakespeare's birth and death day. Just over a year later, at the instigation of Margaret Macmillan and Millicent Mackenzie, Rudolf Steiner was invited to give a series of fourteen lectures at Ilkley, Yorkshire, as part of the conference of the "Educational Union for the Realization of Spiritual Values in Education." It was on this occasion that

Rudolf Steiner gave a special Sunday address on human history in connection with the Trinity. An exhibition of students' work from the Waldorf school had been organized together with a eurythmy performance by students at King's Langley, the fledgling school that was to develop later into a Waldorf school.

The next public lecture was given on August 10 at a teacher training college at Bingley, some eighteen miles south of Ilkley.

The two public lectures given in November 1923 took place during a most important conference in The Hague, which marked the foundation of the Anthroposophical Society in Holland. In lectures, Rudolf Steiner was markedly outspoken about the spiritual background of the education. At the end of the second lecture, he further drew attention to the fact that the art of education should prompt teachers to take on their own education, their self-development, and that only the self-education of teachers could be the seed for what they could give to their students. Nothing can be achieved for the students except what comes forth from the self-education of the teachers. This should be inscribed upon the hearts and souls of all those who wish to teach in a worthy manner.

Early in August 1924, Rudolf Steiner traveled with most of the members of the newly formed Executive Council of the Anthroposophical Society, accompanied by a number of eurythmists, to Paris and then by boat from Boulogne to Great Britain. The Second International Summer School, held at Torquay, was the initiative of D.N. Dunlop and Eleanor Merry. The conference was entitled, "True and False Paths of Spiritual Investigation." During this conference, Rudolf Steiner visited Tintagel, where ruins of King Arthur's castle can be found to this day.

At the end of the conference, Rudolf Steiner traveled to London, gave some lectures to members of the Anthroposophical

Society, and addressed physicians and medical students on the therapeutic methods arising out of spiritual science.

On August 29, Rudolf Steiner spoke in the home of Dr. Larkins, 75 Harley Street, London, at the invitation of Professor Mackenzie. There Rudolf Steiner gave the first of his two London lectures on pedagogy. The second lecture, given the next day and opened to a wider public, was held at Essex Hall. It contains some fine images and speaks of how important it is not to define but rather to characterize a subject imaginatively, so that the child can grow into concepts in a living way. Just as one would not buy a three-year-old child shoes and expect them still to be worn at age nine, so the concepts that we provide in education must grow with the growing understanding of the child.

Here also, he emphasizes the importance in education of truth, goodness, and beauty. Finally, he characterizes three aspects of the education born out of anthroposophy: It is a formative education before the change of teeth, an enlivening education between the change of teeth and puberty, and an awakening education after puberty.

In Torquay in the summer of 1924, Rudolf Steiner also gave seven lectures on the "kingdom of childhood." Together with the lectures in London, the final preparation had now been made for the founding of the first Waldorf school in the English-speaking world, in January 1925, just a few months after Rudolf Steiner's visit to England, and shortly before his death.

Although a vast proportion of Steiner's lectures on education are available in English, the publishers should be congratulated for making the two volumes of public lectures given by Steiner from February 1921 through August 1924 accessible to an English-speaking readership.

R. M. Querido, Ll.D.
Boulder, Colorado

1

Education and Teaching

LONDON — NOVEMBER 19, 1922

Anthroposophy, as I have described it for the past two days, is not just a theoretical view intended to help people get past the sorrows, misfortunes, and pains of life, enabling them to escape into a mystical world.[1] Anthroposophy can help people in practical life. It is connected with the practical questions of existence for the simple reason that the knowledge of which I spoke yesterday and the day before is intended to lead to a genuine penetration, to an accurate view, of the spiritual world. That viewpoint does not, in itself, lead to a life cut off from reality, but actually becomes part of all material events. When we look at a living human being, we are faced not only with what we see, what we understand through speech, and perhaps everything else that person's being expresses that we can perceive with normal consciousness; we also confront the spiritual being living in that person, the spiritual, supersensible being that continually affects that individual's material body.

---

1. See "First Steps in Supersensible Perception and the Relationship of Anthroposophy to Christianity," and "The Relationship of Anthroposophy to Christianity" in *First Steps in Supersensible Perception*, Anthroposophic Publishing Co., London, 1949. Three other lectures in that course are available as *Spiritual Relations in the Human Organism*, Mercury Press, Spring Valley, NY, 1984 (GA 218).

We can never comprehend very much of the world through the knowledge we gain through normal sense perceptions and the intellect connected with those perceptions. People delude themselves into thinking that, when we someday perfect conventional science, we will comprehend more of the world through our intelligence, sense perceptions, and experiments. However, those who are able to consider the relationship between the human being and the world as described in my two earlier lectures know that we can understand only the mineral kingdom through sense perception and intellect. Even when we limit ourselves to the plant kingdom, we must understand that our intellect and senses cannot comprehend the very subtle cosmic rhythms and forces that affect the plant kingdom. That is even more true of the animal kingdom and truer still for human beings. The physical constitution of plants (the least so), animals, and human beings is such that the forces active within them act on their substance like ideal magic. People delude themselves when they believe we can perform the same kinds of laboratory experiments on animals or human beings that we perform on minerals. The purely physical processes that occur in animal and human organisms are caught in an ideal magic. We can gain some understanding of human beings if we can penetrate that ideal magic, that is, if we can look at human beings so that we see through material processes into the continuous inner spiritual activity.

We can achieve insight into spiritual magic only through the understanding I spoke of yesterday and the day before. I showed that one of the first stages of understanding human beings indicates that people not only have a relationship to the world in the moment, but that they can move themselves back to any age they have passed through since their earthly birth. You can place yourself back into a time when you were eighteen or fifteen years old and experience what you experienced then. You can experience it not only as shadowy memories, but with the intensity and strength that existed for you at the time it occurred. You thus become fifteen or twelve years old or whatever again. You undergo a spiritual metamorphosis through this process. In doing so, you can perceive a second organism in the human being, a more subtle organism we call etheric because it has neither weight nor spatial dimensions. That more subtle organism is an organism of time. You have before you everything the etheric organism experienced in time. Nevertheless, you can recognize an organism is before you and learn to understand that the human being exists in that more subtle time organism in just the same way he or she exists in the spatial organism.

If you notice someone is suffering a headache, for example, then perhaps you could say a cure could be achieved by acting on some internal physical organ. You would not need to seek the cure by simply treating the head. We might cure it by treating an organ far from the head. In the spatial organism everything we carry with us is interconnected, and the time organism is the same. The time organism is particularly active in early childhood, but is continually active throughout life in much the following way: Suppose someone has an opportunity at age thirty-five to enter a new situation. If that person meets the situation by doing what is right, then such a person may become aware that at around age twelve important things were learned that now make it possible to move quickly into this new situation.

A certain kind of joy occurs at age thirty-five that arises from the interaction that person had as a child with a teacher. What occurred in that etheric body of eight or ten years old, due to the teacher and the instruction given to the child, acts exactly the same way that our treatment of an organ far from the head acts to cure the headache. Thus, the experiences of a young child affect the thirty-five-year-old person later and create a joyful mood or depression. The entire disposition of an adult depends on what the teacher developed in the etheric body of that adult as a child, in just the same way that one organ of the human spatial body depends upon all the others.

If you think about it, you would say that knowledge of how the etheric body develops, about the relationships of its individual aspects, is certainly the proper basis for educating children. If you think it through fully and conclusively, you must admit that, just as a painter or other artist must learn the techniques of their art, teachers must acquire an understanding of the technique of teaching in an ideal sense. A painter must look, not in the way a layman would, at forms, colors, and their harmonies and disharmonies, and the painter must work out the correct way to handle paints and colored pencils from such observations. A painter's ability to observe properly forms the basis for what must be learned and will permeate his or her entire being. Likewise, a teacher must learn to use the spiritual observation of human beings, to observe what acts on them and unites the entire course of their lives. Teaching cannot be a science, it must be an art. In art, you must first learn a particular capacity for observing, and second learn how to use what you acquire through continuous observation in your continuous struggles with your medium. It is the same with the spiritual science I refer to here, namely, anthroposophical spiritual science that can provide a foundation for a real and true art of education.

Anthroposophy is also basic in another sense. If education is to be truly effective, it must care properly for what will develop from deep within the essence of a young person. Teachers must be able to accept a child as a divine moral task bestowed on them. As teachers, the things that elevate our moral relationship to teaching and permeate our educational activity with a kind of religious meditation, give us the necessary strength to act alongside the children and work with all the inner characteristics that need development. In other words, all educational activities must themselves be moral acts, and they must arise from moral impulses. We must use these moral impulses within the context of the human understanding and human observation just described.

When we consider these things, we will, of course, see how people's lives clearly progress in developmental stages—much more so than people ordinarily think. People usually observe only superficially, for instance, that children get a second set of teeth when they are about seven years old. People often see the bodily symptoms accompanying that change, but do not look more closely at the transformations occurring in the child during such a change. People who can properly observe a child, before and after the age of seven, can see that, after seven, forces that were previously hidden develop out of the depths of the human being. If we look at things properly, then we must admit that the change of teeth is not simply a one-time, sudden event in human life. The change of teeth at age seven, although we do not repeat it, is something that occurs throughout the period between the time the child receives his or her first teeth until the change of teeth. During that whole time, forces in the human organism are pushing and shoving, and result in the second set of teeth breaking through. The change of teeth simply concludes the processes active during the child's first period of life. Children do not change teeth ever again, but what does that mean? That means that until age seven, children develop those forces in their physical body that are needed to grow a second set of teeth, but those children will not change teeth again and now no longer need such forces. The question is, what becomes of those forces?

If we look supersensibly at a human being, we can again recognize those forces in the transformed life of the child's soul between the change of teeth and puberty. The child's soul is then different. A different capacity for learning has been added to the soul, and the child has a different orientation toward the surroundings. If we see things spiritually and not just physically, then the situation is different. We can then understand that what we can see in the child's soul from approximately ages seven to fourteen existed previously in the child's physical organism. Earlier, it was an activity connected with the process inducing the change of teeth, but at age seven it ceases to be physically active and begins to be active in the soul.

Thus, if you want to understand the forces active in the child's soul between the change of teeth and puberty, you must look at the physical activities between birth until the change of teeth. The forces now active in the child's soul then acted on the physical body. The result is that when we observe properly, we can see that, in a more subtle sense, the young child is entirely a sense organ. That is true particularly of a baby, but in a certain way still true right until the change of teeth. In a subtle way, a baby is a kind of groping eye. The way the eye looks at things and recreates what exists outside so the child has an inner picture of the external object, gives the child in earliest life a perception, but not a visual picture.

The baby is in its entirety a sense organ, and perhaps I can illustrate this. Let us think of a baby. As adults, we have our sense of taste in the tongue and gums. However, as spiritual science shows us, the baby has a hint of taste throughout the entire body. The baby is an organ of taste throughout. The baby as a whole is also an organ of smell and, more inwardly, an organ of touch. The entire constitution of the baby is sense-like in its nature, and this sense-like nature radiates throughout the whole body. For that reason, until age seven the child tends to recreate inwardly everything happening in the surroundings and to develop accordingly. If you observe children with your more subtle senses and with spiritual-scientific understanding, you will see that they recreate every gesture made in their surroundings, and they attempt to do what people do in their presence. You will thus see that the child is an imitative being until the change of teeth. The most important capacity of the young child becomes apparent from this imitative behavior. The most important capacity is the development of speech. That depends entirely on the fact that children live into what people in their surroundings do and develop speech through imitation—that is, through inwardly conforming to what occurs in their surroundings. Thus, as teachers, when we work with children during their first stage of life, we need to recognize imitation as the most important aspect of teaching. We can teach a very young child only by creating an environment filled with those activities and processes the child should imitate to gain strength in spirit, soul, and body; those things we implant not only in children's spirits and souls, but also in their bodies, and the way they strengthen the inner organs remain as the children's constitution throughout life. How I act around a child of four remains with that person into old age. Thus, my behavior determines, in a way, the child's fate in later life.

That can be illustrated with an example. Sometimes people come to you when you work in this field and say, for example, that their child was always a good child and never did anything wrong, but the child has now done something terrible. If you ask in detail what occurred, you might hear that the child stole some money from the mother. If you are adept at such things, you might ask how old the child is, and receive the reply, "Five." Thus, such activity is based primarily on imitation. You will then learn that the child had seen the mother take money from the cupboard every day. The child simply imitated and was not concerned with good or evil. The child only imitated what was seen at home. If we believe we can achieve anything by instructing the child about good and evil, we only delude ourselves. We can educate very young children only when we present them with examples they can imitate, including thoughts. A subtle spiritual connection exists between children and those who raise them. When we are with children, we should be careful to harbor only thoughts and feelings they can imitate in their own thoughts and feelings. In their souls, young children are entirely sense receptors and perceive things so subtle that we as adults could not dream they even occur.

After the change of teeth, forces lying deep within the child become forces of the soul. Earlier, children are devoted entirely to their surroundings; but now they can stand as one soul to another and can, compared to their earlier imitative behavior, accept authority as a matter of course. During earliest childhood until the change of teeth, our real desire is to be totally integrated into our surroundings, which is, in a sense, the physical manifestation of religious feeling. Religious feelings are a spiritual devotion to the spirit; the child devotes the physical body to the physical surroundings. That is the physical counterpart of religion.

After the age of seven, children no longer devote the physical body to their physical surroundings; rather, they devote the soul to other souls. A teacher steps forward to help the child, and the child needs to see the teacher as the source of the knowledge of everything good and evil. At this point children are just as devoted to what the teacher says and develops within the children as they were earlier to the gestures and activities around them. Between seven and fourteen years of age, an urge arises within children to devote themselves to natural authority. Children thus want to become what that authority is. The love of that natural authority and a desire to please now become the main principle, just as imitation was earlier.

You would hardly believe that someone like myself, who in the early 1890s wrote *The Philosophy of Freedom*, would support an unjustified principle of authority.[2] What I mean is something like natural law. From approximately ages seven to fourteen, children view their teacher in such a way that they have no intellectual comprehension of "this is good or true or evil or false or ugly," but rather, "this is good because the teacher says it is good," or "this is beautiful because the teacher says it is beautiful." We must bring all the secrets of the world to the child through the indirect path of the beloved teacher. That is the principle of human development from around the age of seven until fourteen.

We can therefore say that a religious-like devotion toward the physical surroundings fills a child during the first years of life. From the change of teeth until puberty, an esthetic comprehension of the surroundings fills the child, a comprehension permeated with love. Children expect pleasure with everything the teacher presents to them and displeasure from whatever the teacher withholds. Everything that acts educationally during this period should enter the child's inner perspective. We may conclude that, whereas during the first stage of life the teacher should be an example, during the second period the teacher should be an authority in the most noble sense—a natural authority due to qualities of character. As teachers, we will then have within us what children need, in a sense, to properly educate themselves. The most important aspect of self-education is moral education. I will speak more of that when the first part of my lecture has been translated.

---

2. *The Philosophy of Freedom*, later called *The Philosophy of Spiritual Activity*, is now translated as *Intuitive Thinking as a Spiritual Path: A Philosophy of Freedom*, Anthroposophic Press, Hudson, NY, 1995.

(At this point, Rudolf Steiner paused so that George Adams could deliver the first part of this lecture in English.)

When we say children are entirely sense organs before the age of seven, we must understand that, after the change of teeth, that is, after the age of seven, children's sense-perceptive capacities have moved more toward the surface of the body and moved away from their inner nature. Children's sense impressions, however, still cannot effectively enter the sense organs in an organized and regulated way. We see that from the change of teeth until puberty, therefore, the child's nature is such that the child harbors in the soul a devotion to sense perceptions, but the child's inner will is incapable of affecting them.

Human intellect creates an inner participation in sense perception, but we are intellectual beings only after puberty. Our relationship to the world is appropriate for judging it intellectually only after puberty. To reason intellectually means to reason from personal inner freedom, but we can do this only after puberty. Thus, from the change of teeth until puberty we should not educate children in an intellectual way, and we should not moralize intellectually. During the first seven years of life, children need what they can imitate in their sense-perceptible reality. After that, children want to hear from their educational authority what they can and cannot do, what they should consider to be true or untrue, just or unjust and so forth.

Something important begins to stir in the child around the age of nine or ten. Teachers who can truly observe children know that, at about the age of nine or ten, children have a particularly strong need. Then, although children do not have intellectualized doubts, they do have a kind of inner unrest; a kind of inner question, a childlike question concerning fate they cannot express and, indeed, do not yet need to express.

Children feel this in a kind of half sleep, in an unconscious way. You need only look with the proper eye to see how children develop during this period. I think you know exactly what I am referring to here—namely, that children want something special from the teacher whom they look up to with love. Ordinarily, you cannot answer that desire the way you would answer an intellectually posed question. It is important during this time that you develop an intense and intimate, trusting relationship so that what arises in the children is a feeling that you as teacher particularly care for and love them.

The answer to children's most important life question lies in their perception of love and their trust in the teacher. What is the actual content of that question? As I said, children do not ask through reasoning, but through feeling, subconsciously. We can formulate things children cannot, and we can say, therefore, that children at that stage are still naïve and accept the authority of the beloved teacher without question. However, now a certain need awakens in the child. The child needs to feel what is good and what is evil differently, as though they exist in the world as forces.

Until this time, children looked up to the teacher, in a sense, but now they want to see the world through the teacher's eyes. Children not only want to know that the teacher is a human being who says something is good or bad, they also want to feel that the teacher speaks as a messenger of the Spirit, a messenger of God, and knows something from the higher worlds. As I said, children do not say it through reasoning, but they feel it. The particular question arising in the child's feeling will tell you that a certain thing is appropriate for that child. It will be apparent that your statement that something is good or bad has very deep roots, and, thus, the child will gain renewed trust.

That is also the point in moral education where we can begin to move away from simple imitative behavior or saying something is good or bad. At about the age of nine or ten, we can begin to show morality pictorially, because children are still sense oriented and without reasoning. We should educate children pictorially—that is, through pictures, pictures for all the senses—during the entire period of elementary school, between the change of teeth and puberty. Even though children at that age may not be completely sense oriented, they still live in their senses, which are now more recognizable at the surface of the body.

Tomorrow evening I will discuss how to teach children from the age of six or seven through the time when they learn to read or write. Right now I want to consider only the moral side of education.

When children have reached age nine or ten, we may begin to present pictures that primarily stimulate the imagination. We may present pictures of good people, pictures that awaken a feeling of sympathy for what people do. Please take note that I did not say we should lecture children about moral commandments. I did not say we should approach children's intellect with moral reasoning. We should approach children through esthetics and imagination. We should awaken a pleasure or displeasure of good and bad things, of just or unjust things, of high ideals, of moral action, and of things that occur in the world to balance incorrect action. Whereas previously we needed to place ourselves before the children as a kind of moral regulator, we now need to provide them with pictures that do no more than affect the imagination living within their sense nature. Before puberty, children should receive morality as a feeling. They should receive a firm feeling that, "Something is good, and I can be sympathetic toward it," or "I should feel antipathy toward something bad." Sympathies and antipathies, that is, judgments within feelings, should be the basis of what is moral.

If you recognize, in the way I have presented it, that everything in the human time organism is interconnected, then you will also recognize that it is important for the child that you do the right things at the right time. You cannot get a plant to grow in a way that it immediately flowers; blooming occurs later. First, you must tend the roots. Should you want to make the roots bloom, you would be attempting something ridiculous. Similarly, it would be just as ridiculous to want to present intellectually formulated moral judgments to the child between the change of teeth and puberty. You must first tend the seed and the root—that is, a feeling for morality. When children have a feeling for morality, their intelligence will awaken after puberty. What they have gained in feeling during that period will then continue into an inner development afterward. Moral and intellectual reasoning will awaken on their own. It is important that we base all moral education on that.

You cannot make a plant's root blossom; you must wait until the root develops into the plant and then the plant blossoms. In the same way, you must, in a sense, tend the moral root in the feeling and develop sympathy for what is moral. You must then allow children to carry that feeling into their intellect through their own forces as human beings. Later in life they will have the deep inner satisfaction of knowing that something more lives within them than just memories of what their teacher said was right or wrong. Instead, an inner joy will fill their entire soul life from the knowledge that moral judgment awoke within them at the proper time. That we do not slavishly educate children in a particular moral direction, rather, we prepare them so that their own free developing souls can grow and blossom in a moral direction, strengthens people not only with a capacity for moral judgment, but also gives them a moral strength. When we want a spiritual foundation for education, this fact reminds us again and again that we must bring everything to developing children in the proper way and at the proper time.

Now you might ask: If one should not provide commandments that appeal to the intellect, what should you appeal to when you want to implant a feeling for moral reasoning in the school-age child? Well, authority in its own right certainly does lead to intangible things in the relationship between the teacher and the child! I would like to illustrate this through an example. I can teach children pictorially—that is, non-intellectually—about the immortality of the human soul. Until the time of puberty, the intellect is actually absent in the child. I must interweave nature and spirit, and thus what I tell the children is fashioned into an artistic picture: "Look at this butterfly's cocoon. The butterfly crawls out of the cocoon. In just the same way, the soul comes out of the human body when the body dies." In this way, I can stimulate the children's imagination and bring a living, moral picture to their souls. I can do that in two ways. I could say to myself: I am a mature teacher and tremendously wise. The children are small and extremely ignorant, and since they have not yet elevated themselves to my stature, I need to create a picture for them. I create a picture for them, even though I know it has little value for myself. If I were to say that to myself, and bring a picture to the children with that attitude, it would not act on their souls. It would just pass quickly through their souls, since intangible relationships exist between the teacher and child. However, I could say to myself: I am really not much wiser than the children, or they are, at least subconsciously, even wiser than I—that is, I could respect the children. Then I could say to myself: I did not create that picture myself; nature gave us the picture of the butterfly creeping from its cocoon. And then, I believe in that picture just as intensely as I want the children to believe. If I have the strength of my own beliefs within me, then the picture remains fixed in the children's souls, and the things that will live do not lie in the coarseness of the world, but in the subtleties that exist between the teacher and child.

The incomprehensible things that play between teacher and child richly replace everything we could transfer through an intellectual approach. In this manner, children gain an opportunity to freely develop themselves alongside the teacher. The teacher can say: I live in the children's surroundings and must, therefore, create those opportunities through which they can develop themselves to the greatest possible extent. To do this I must stand next to the children without feeling superior, and recognize that I am only a human being who is a few years older.

In a relative sense we are not always wiser, and we therefore do not always need to feel superior to children. We should be helpers for their development. If you tend plants as a gardener, you certainly do not make the sap move from the root to the flower. Rather, you prepare the plant's environment so that the flow of sap can develop. As teachers we must be just as selfless so that the child's inner forces can unfold. Then we will be good teachers, and the children can flourish in the proper way.

(*Rudolf Steiner paused again to allow the second part of the lecture to be translated for the audience.*)

When we develop morality in the human being in that way, it then develops just as one thing develops from another in the plant. At first, humanly appropriate moral development arises from the imitative desires within the human organism. As I already described, morality gains a certain firmness so that people have the necessary inner strength later in life, a strength anchored in the physical organism, for moral certainty. Otherwise, people may be physically weak and unable to follow their moral impulses, however good they may be. If the moral example acts strongly and intensely on the child during the first period of childhood, then a moral fortitude develops. If children, from the change of teeth until puberty, can properly take hold of the forces of sympathy and antipathy for good and against evil, then later they will have the proper moral stance regarding the uncertainties that might keep them from doing what is morally necessary. Through imitation, children will develop within their organism what their souls need, so that their moral feelings and perceptions, their sympathies and antipathies, can properly develop during the second period of childhood. The capacity for intellectual moral judgment awakens in the third period of the child's development, which is oriented toward the spirit. This occurs as surely as the plant in the light of the Sun blossoms and fruits. Morality can only take firm root in the spirit if the body and soul have been properly prepared. It can then freely awaken to life, just as the blossom and fruit freely awaken in the plant in the light of the Sun.

When we develop morality in human beings while respecting their inner freedom, then the moral impulse connects with their inner being so that they can truly feel it is something that belongs to them. They feel the same way toward their moral strength and moral actions as they do toward the forces of growth within their body, toward the circulation of their own blood. People will feel about the morality developed within themselves in the proper manner as they feel about the natural forces of life throughout their bodies, that they pulse and strengthen them right up to the surface of the skin.

What happens then? People realize that if they are immoral, they are deformed. They feel disfigured in the same way they would feel if they were physically missing a limb. Through the moral development I have described, people learn. They come to say to themselves that if they are not filled with morality, and if their actions are not permeated with morality, then they are deformed human beings.

The strongest moral motive we can possibly develop within human beings is the feeling that they are disfigured if they are immoral. People only need proper development and then they will be whole. If you help develop people so that they want to be whole human beings, they will of themselves develop an inner tendency toward the spiritual due to this approach to morality. They will then see the good that flows through the world and that it acts within them just as effectively as the forces of nature act within their bodies. To put it pictorially, they will then understand that if they see a horseshoe-shaped piece of iron, someone might then come along and say we could use that horseshoe as a magnet because it has its own inner forces. But, another might say that it is only iron and is unimportant, and would use it to shoe a horse. Someone who sees things in the latter way could not, due to the way their life developed, see that spiritual life exists within the human being. Someone who only sees the superficial, and not how the spirit acts and interacts within the human being, is the kind of person who would shoe a horse with a horseshoe-shaped piece of magnetic iron. In such a case, the person has not been educated to see life properly and to develop the proper strengths. When comprehended spiritually, a proper education, felt and brought to the will, is the strongest motive for social activity.

Today, we are standing under the star of the social problem. This problem exists for a reason, and I would be happy to say more about it, but my time is now coming to an end. However, I would like to mention that the social problems of today have many aspects, and much is needed to approach these questions in all detail. Modern people who look at things objectively want much for the future of humanity and for reforming social life. However, everything we can think of and create in practice for our institutions, everything we can think of in the way of schemes or about the nature of modern social life, demonstrates to those who see morality in the light of spirituality that dealing with today's social problems without including the question of morality is like hunting for something in a dark room.

We can bring the social question into proper perspective only through a genuine comprehension of morality. Anyone who looks at life with an eye toward the comprehensive connections found there would say that morality is the light that must enlighten social life if we are to see the social questions in a truly human way. Modern people, therefore, need to gain an understanding of the moral question connected with the social question. I believe that it is perhaps possible to show that what I have called spiritual science, or anthroposophy, wants to tackle the great questions of our times, and that it has earnest intentions regarding the questions of morality and developing morality within human beings.

(*George Adams completed his English translation of the lecture.*)

Rudolf Steiner on "ideal magic," from lecture of November 17, 1922 (see footnote, page 1):

Along with exact clairvoyance, you must also achieve something I refer to as *ideal magic*. This is a kind of magic that must be differentiated from the false magic practiced externally, and associated with many charlatans. You must certainly differentiate that from what I mean by *ideal magic*.

What I mean by ideal magic is the following: when someone looks back over life with ordinary consciousness, one will see how, from year to year and from decade to decade, one has changed in a certain sense. Such a person would see that habits have changed, however slowly. One gains certain capacities while others disappear. If one looks honestly at the capacities that exist during earthly life, one would have to say that, over time, one becomes someone else. Life causes that to happen. We are completely devoted to life and life educates us, trains us and forms the soul.

If, however, people want to enter the spiritual world—in other words, want to attain *ideal magic*—they must not only intensify inner thinking so that they recognize a second level of existence, as I previously described, but they must also free their will from its connection to the physical body. Ordinarily, we can activate the will only by using the physical body—the legs, arms, or the organs of speech. The physical body is the basis for our will. However, we can do the following: as spiritual researchers we must carry out exercises of the will in a very systematic way to achieve ideal magic along with exact clairvoyance. Such a person must, for example, develop the will so strongly that, at a particular point in life, one recognizes that a specific habit must be broken and replaced with another in the soul.

You will need many years, but if you energetically use your will to transform certain experiences in the way I described, it is nevertheless possible. Thus, you can, as it were, go beyond allowing only the physical body to be your teacher and replace that kind of development with self-discipline.

Through energetic exercise of the will, such as I have described in my books, you will become an initiate in a modern sense, and no longer merely re-experience in sleep what you experience during the day. You will achieve a state that is not sleep, but that can be experienced in complete consciousness. This state provides you with the opportunity to be active while you sleep—that is, the opportunity while you are outside your body to not merely remain passive in the spiritual world, as is normally the case. Rather, you can act in the spirit world; you can be active in the spiritual world. During sleep, people are ordinarily unable to move forward, to progress. However, those who are modern initiates, in the sense I have described, have the capacity to be active as a human being in the life that exists between falling asleep and waking up. If you bring your will into the state in which you live outside your body, then you can develop your consciousness in a much different way. You will be able to develop consciousness in a way that you can see what people experience in the period directly following death. Through this other kind of consciousness, you can experience what occurs during the period after earthly life, just as you will be able to see what occurs in pre-earthly life. You can see how you pass through a life of existence in the spiritual world just as you go through life in the physical world during earthly existence. You recognize yourself as a pure spirit in the spiritual world just as you can recognize yourself as a physical body within the physical world. Thus, you have the opportunity to create a judgment about how long life lasts during what I would refer to as the time of moral evaluation.

2

The Art of Teaching from
an Understanding of the Human Being

LONDON — NOVEMBER 20, 1922

It might seem unusual to speak about practical questions in education from the standpoint of a particular philosophy—that is, anthroposophy. In this case, however, the reason for speaking about education arises from the practice of teaching itself.

As you know, I will speak tonight of the way of teaching being practiced at the Waldorf school in Stuttgart. The pedagogical ideas and goals proposed through anthroposophy have been, for the most part, established at the Waldorf school. A few years ago everyone was talking about problems in education, and industrialist Emil Molt decided to create a school for the children of the workers in his factory. He turned to me to provide the pedagogical content and direction for that school.[1]

At first, we dealt only with a particular group of children who came from a particular class—proletarian children connected with the Waldorf Company and with some children whose parents were members of the Anthroposophical Society. However, we soon extended the task of the school. We began originally

---

1. Emil Molt (1876–1936), from Schwäbisch Gmünd in southern Germany, was the owner of the Waldorf Astoria cigarette factory, from which Waldorf education derives its name.

with about 150 children in eight classes, but we now have eleven classes and over 700 children. Before that, a group of friends within the circle of anthroposophy made a trip to Dornach, Switzerland to attend a conference on education at the Goetheanum at Christmas. As a result, I was invited to lecture at Oxford this past August. Following the Oxford lectures, the Educational Union formed in order to bring the educational principles I will discuss today to a greater application in England.

I need to mention these circumstances so you will not think our discussion this evening is to be theoretical. You should realize that I want to speak about a genuinely practical manner of educating. I need to emphasize this also because this evening we will, of course, be able to mention only a few things. Those things I can bring up will also be rather incomplete compared to the reality of those principles of education, since they are not about "programs" but about practice. When we speak of practice, we can only speak in terms of examples taken from that practice. It is much easier to talk about a program, since you can speak in generalities and about general principles. We cannot do that when speaking of the Waldorf school education due to its own distinctive characteristics. As I mentioned before, our concern is to begin pedagogy and education derived from a spiritual-scientific perspective, a perspective that can lead us to a true comprehension of the human being, and thus to a true comprehension of the nature of a child.

Painters or other artists must learn two things in order to practice their art. In the case of painters, they must first learn a particular skill for observing form and color. The artist must be able to create from the nature of form and color and cannot begin with some theoretical comprehension of them. The artist can begin only by living within the nature of form and color. Only then can the artist learn the second thing, namely, technique. Spiritual science does not comprehend education as an academic or theoretical field. Spiritual science sees it as a genuine art, as an art that uses the most noble material found in the world—human beings. Education is concerned with children who reveal so marvelously to us the deepest riddles of the cosmos. Children allow us to observe from year to year, even from week to week, how physiognomy, gestures, and everything else they express reveal spirit and soul as a divine gift of the spiritual worlds hidden deep within them. The perspective I am speaking of assumes that, just as the painter must learn to properly observe how form and color—the activity arising through the hands, soul, and spirit—result from that understanding, so the artist in teaching must be able to follow the essence of the human being revealed in the child. However, this is not possible if you do not elevate your capacity to observe above the level of common consciousness—that is, if you cannot gain a true observation of soul and spiritual activities in life. That is precisely the objective of anthroposophy. What contemporary people typically call "cognition" addresses only the corporeal—that is, what speaks to the senses. If people have not risen to a genuine comprehension of the spirit, how can they learn to understand the soul? They can gain understanding of the soul only by understanding the expressions and activities of their own soul. Through self-observation, they learn about their own thinking, about their own feeling and willing. Those are aspects of the soul. They comprehend the soul only through reasoning. The senses perceive the sense perceptible. However, such people can understand the soul only by forming a judgment about those characteristics within themselves and then concluding that they have something like a soul.

Anthroposophy does not begin with that ordinary way of thinking. Instead, it seeks to systematically develop those forces sleeping within the human soul so that (don't be surprised by my expression) a kind of *precise clairvoyance* results. With precise clairvoyance, you can penetrate the characteristics of the soul to see what is truly the soul. You can perceive the soul through that spiritual vision just as you can recognize colors through the eyes or tones through the ears. Through normal consciousness we can comprehend the spirit active in the world only as a conclusion. If we insist on remaining within normal consciousness, then we can say that we see only the phenomena of nature or of the soul. From that, we conclude that a spiritual foundation exists. Our thinking concludes that spirit and soul are at the foundation of what exists physically. Anthroposophy develops forces sleeping in the soul, organs of spiritual perception through which we can experience the spirit through living thinking, not merely as a conclusion.

You can have a genuine understanding of the human being only when you have seen the soul, and when you can experience the spirit in living thought. A living understanding of the human being arises that can permeate you through spiritual science, so that you can see in every moment of the developing child's life how the spirit and soul act in the child. You do not see the child only from outside through the senses; you see also the sense perceptible expression of the soul. You do not work with just a revelation of the soul, but with the actual substance of the soul that you can see, just as your eyes see colors. You can begin with how spirit works within the child because, through anthroposophy, you can understand how to comprehend spirit with living thought.

Thus, the art of teaching I am speaking of here begins with a living comprehension of the human being, along with a comprehension of the development taking place in the child at every moment of life. When you understand in that way how the material we work with in teaching is the most noble, when you recognize how your teaching can affect the human being, then you can see many things differently than possible through ordinary consciousness. You can then teach and give educational guidance based on that knowledge. You can, through direct practical interaction with the child, develop what you can see in the soul and experience in the spirit.

Observation that is truly alive shows that spirit exists within the child no less than in the adult. However, that spirit lies hidden deep within the child and must first conquer the body. If we can see that spirit before it speaks to us through language or reveals itself through intellectual thought, we can receive an impression of the marvelous way spirit's divine gift affects the child's organism. You will then get an impression of why we certainly cannot say that the physical nature of the human being is one thing, and spirit another. In children you can see how spirit, much more so than with adults, works directly on the physical—that is, how spirit completely permeates the physical. As adults, we have spirit to the extent that we need to think about the world. Children, on the other hand, have spirit to the extent that they need to form their organism through spiritual sculpting. Much more than people believe, the human physical organism throughout all of earthly life is the result of how that spirit hidden within the child develops the physical organism. To avoid speaking abstractly, I would like to present some concrete examples.

If you look at a child only as conventional science does, so that you only perceive what ordinary physiology presents through dissection—that is, if you do not have a spiritual view of the child—you will not see the effect of all the different events on the child's physical organism. For instance, the child does something and is shouted at by an adult. That makes a very different impression on the child than it would on an adult, if one were to shout at the adult. We must remember that a child functions very differently than an adult. The adult's sense organs exist on the surface of the body. Adults can control with their intellect what comes through the sense organs. Adults can form fully developed will from within when confronted with sense impressions. However, the child is completely surrendered to the external world. If I may express it pictorially (but I mean this to a certain degree in a literal sense), the child is entirely a sense organ. Allow me to be very clear about this. Look at an infant. If we look with an external understanding at an infant, it appears that the baby feels and sees the world just as an adult does, except that the infant's intellect and will are not as well developed as in adults. That is, however, not the case at all. Adults feel taste only on their tongue and gums. What takes place only at the surface in adults permeates the child's organism right into the innermost depths. In a way, children perceive taste throughout their bodies when they eat. They perceive light throughout themselves when light and colors enter their eyes. That is not simply pictorial; this is actually how it is. When light shines on children, the light vibrates not only in their nervous system, it also vibrates in their breathing and throughout their circulatory system. Light vibrates throughout the entirety of the child's organism in just the same way light acts within the adult's eye only. The child is, throughout the entire body, a sensing organ. Just as the eye is completely occupied with the world and lives entirely in light, children live entirely in their surroundings. Children carry spirit within themselves in order to absorb everything that lives in their physical surroundings into their entire organism. Because of this, when we yell at a child, our yelling places the entire body into a particular kind of activity. When we yell at a child, a certain inner vibration occurs that is much stronger than that in an adult, who can make certain inner counteractions. What happens then is a kind of stopping short of the spiritual and soul life, which affects the child's physical body directly. Thus, when we often yell at and frighten a child, we affect not only the child's soul, but the child's entire physical body. Depending on how we act around children, we can affect the health of human beings all the way into the final years of old age.

The most important means of teaching a very young child is through the way we, as adults, act when in the child's presence. If children experience a continuous hustle and bustle, a continuous hastiness in their environment, then they will take up an inner tendency toward haste within their physical body. If you truly understand human beings so that you can observe their spirit and soul, you can see in children of eleven or twelve whether they were brought up in a restless or hurried environment, in a more appropriate environment, or in one where everything moved too slowly. We can see it in the way they walk. If the child was brought up in a hurried environment, one where everything proceeded with extreme restlessness, one where impressions continually changed, then the child will walk with a light step. The kind of environment the child had makes an impression on the child, even in the way of walking, in the step. If a child had insufficient stimulus in the surroundings so that continuous boredom was experienced, we see the reverse in how the child walks in later life with a heavy step. I mention these examples because they are particularly visible, and because they show how we can observe people better. Through this example, you can see what we are able to give to children when we see them properly in early childhood. During early childhood, children imitate their surroundings. They are particularly imitative in learning what they should do in their souls—that is, what is moral. I would like to give an example of this as well.

Those who have had to deal with such things can also experience them. For example, a father once came to me and said that his son had always been a good boy and had always done what the parents had found morally pleasing. But, now he had stolen money. Well, in such a case, anyone who truly understands human nature would ask where the child had taken the money. The father replied, "from the cupboard." I then asked further whether someone removed money from the cupboard every day. "The child's mother," was the reply; thus, the child had seen the mother remove money from the cupboard every day. Young children are imitative beings who dedicate the entire soul to their surroundings, and, therefore, they do what they see happening in the surroundings. The young child does not respond to reprimands, does not respond to "do" and "don't." Such things are not strongly connected with a child's soul. Children do only what they see happening in their surroundings. However, children see things much more exactly than adults do, even though they are unconscious of what it is they see. What children see in their surroundings leaves an imprint on their organism. The entire organism of the child is an imprint of what occurs in the surroundings.

Contemporary understanding overvalues way too much what is called "heredity." When people see the characteristics of some adult, they often say such traits are inherited by purely physical transfer from one generation to another. Those who truly understand human beings, however, see that children's muscles develop according to the impressions from their surroundings. They can see that, depending on whether or not we treat a child with tenderness and care, with love or in some other manner, the child's breathing and circulation develop according to the feelings experienced. If a child often experiences someone approaching with love, who instinctively falls into step with the child and moves at the tempo required by the child's inner nature, then the child will, in subtle ways, develop healthy lungs. If you want to know where the traits for a healthy adult physical body arise from, you must look back to when the child was affected as one great sense organ. You must look at the words, the gestures, and the entire relationship of the child to the surroundings, and how these things affected the child's muscles, circulation, and breathing. You will see that a child imitates not just in learning to speak—which depends entirely on imitation, even into the bodily organization that makes speech possible—but you will see that the child's whole body, particularly in the more subtle aspects of the physical body, reflects what we do in the child's presence.

To the extent that a person's physical body is strong or weak, that the physical body can be depended upon, gratitude or blame for the way one walks through life, even in old age, is due to the impressions made on a person as a small child.

What I just said about growing children being imitative beings applies throughout the first period of childhood, that is, from birth until the change of teeth at approximately age seven. At that time, the child goes through many more changes than is generally thought. In order to build a secure foundation for a genuine art of education and teaching, we need to fully penetrate what occurs in the child's development; that is what I want to discuss in the second part of the lecture after this first part has been translated.

(Rudolf Steiner paused at this point while George Adams delivered the first part of this lecture in English.)

At around age seven, the change of teeth is not just a physical symptom of transformation in human physical nature, but also indicates the complete transformation of the child's soul. The child is primarily an imitative being until the change of teeth. It is in the child's nature to depend on the forces that arise from imitation for the physical body's development.

After approximately age seven and the change of teeth, children no longer need to be physically devoted to their environment, but instead need to be able to be devoted with the soul. Everything that occurs in the child's presence before the change of teeth penetrates the depths of that child's being. What penetrates the child during the second period of life is due to an acceptance of the authority of the child's teachers. The child's desire to learn such adult arts as reading and writing does not arise out of the child's own nature, but expresses the acceptance of that natural authority. It is a tragic pedagogical error if you believe children have any desire to learn those things, things that serve as communication for adults! What actually acts developmentally on a child are the things that arise from the child's loving devotion toward an accepted authority. Children do not learn what they learn for any reason found in the instruction itself. Children learn because they see what an adult knows and is able to do, and because an adult who is the child's accepted educational authority says this or that is something appropriate to be learned. That goes right to the child's moral foundation.

I would remind you that the child learns morality through imitation until the change of teeth. From the age of seven until about fourteen—that is, from the change of teeth until puberty—the child learns everything through loving acceptance of authority. We cannot achieve anything with children through the intellect, that is, with commandments such as "this is good" or "that is evil." Instead, a feeling must grow within the child to discover what is good based on what the accepted authority indicates as good. The child must also learn to feel displeasure with what that accepted authority presents as evil. Children may not have any reason for finding pleasure or displeasure in good or evil things other than those revealed by the authority standing beside them. It is not important that things appear good or evil to the child's intellect, but that they are so for the teacher. This is necessary for true education.

It is important during that period for all morality, including religion, to be presented to the child by other human beings; the human relationship with the teachers is important. Whenever we think we teach children by approaching them through intellectual reasoning, we really teach in a way that merely brings inner death to much within them. Although children at that age are no longer entirely a sense organ, and their sense organs have now risen to the surface of the body, they still have their entire soul within. Children gain nothing through intellectualization, which brings a kind of systemization to the senses, but they can accept what the recognized authority of the teacher brings to them as an ensouled picture.

From the change of teeth until puberty, we must form all our teaching artistically; we must begin everywhere from an artistic perspective. If we teach children letters, from which they are to learn to read and write as is now commonly done, then they will have absolutely no relationship to those characters. We know, of course, that the letters of the alphabet arose in earlier civilizations from a pictorial imitation of external processes in things. Writing began with pictograms. When we teach the letters of the alphabet to the child, we must also begin with pictures. Thus, in our Waldorf school in Stuttgart, we do not begin with letters; we begin with instruction in painting and drawing. That is difficult for a child of six or seven years, just entering school, but we soon overcome the difficulties. We can overcome those difficulties by standing alongside the child with a proper attitude, carried within our authority in such a way that the child does indeed want to imitate what the teacher creates with form and color. The child wants to do the same as the teacher does. Children must learn everything along that indirect path. That is possible only, however, when both an external and an internal relationship exists between the teacher and pupil, which occurs when we fill all our teaching with artistic content. An unfathomable, impenetrable relationship exists between the teacher and child. Mere educational techniques and the sort of things teachers learn are not effective; the teacher's attitude, along with its effect on the feelings of the child, is most effective; the attitude carried within the teacher's soul is effective. You will have the proper attitude in your soul when you as a teacher can perceive the spiritual in the world.

I would like to give you another example to illustrate what I mean. This is an example I particularly like to use. Suppose we want to stimulate the child in a moral-religious way. This would be the proper way to do so for the nine- or ten-year-old. In the kind of education I am describing, you can read from the child's development what you need to teach each year, even each month. Suppose I want to give a child of about nine an idea of the immortality of the human soul. I could tiptoe around it intellectually, but that would not leave a lasting impression on the child. It might even harm the child's soul, because when I give an intellectual presentation about moral-religious issues nothing enters the child's soul. What remains in the child's soul results from intangible things between the teacher and child. However, I can give the child an experience of the immortality of the soul through artistically formed pictures. I could say, "Look at a butterfly's cocoon and how the butterfly breaks through the cocoon. It flies away and moves about in the sunlight. The human soul in the human body is the same as the butterfly in the cocoon. When a human being passes through the gates of death, the soul leaves the body and then moves about in the spiritual world."

Now, you can teach that to children in two ways. You can feel yourself to be above children and think that you are wise and children are dumb. You might feel that children cannot understand what you, in your wisdom, can understand about the immortality of the soul, so you will create a picture for them.

If I make up such a picture for the children while feeling myself to be superior to them, that will make an impression on the children that soon passes, but it leaves a withered place within them. However, I can also approach the child differently, with the attitude that I believe in this picture myself. I can see that I do not simply fabricate the picture, but that divine spiritual powers have placed the butterfly and cocoon into nature. The fluttering of the butterfly out of the cocoon is a real picture within nature and the world of what I should understand as the immortality of the soul. The emergence of the butterfly confronts me with the idea of immortality in a simple and primitive way. It was God Himself who wanted to show me something through that emerging butterfly. Only when I can develop such a belief in my pictures is the invisible and supersensible relationship between the child and myself effective. If I develop my own comprehension with that depth of soul and then give it to the child, that picture takes root in the child and develops further throughout life. If we transform everything into a pictorial form between the change of teeth and puberty, we do not teach the child static concepts that the child will retain unchanged. If we teach children static concepts, it would be the same as if we were to clamp their hands in machines so that they could no longer freely grow. It is important that we teach children inwardly flexible concepts. Such concepts can grow just as our limbs do, so that what we develop within the child can become something very different when the child matures.

Such things can be judged only by those who do not merely look at children and ask what their needs are or what their developmental capacities are. Only those who can survey all of human life can judge these things, which then become a rather intuitive way of teaching. I could give you an example of this.

Suppose we have a school-age child that has inner devotion toward the teacher. I would like to illustrate the strength that could develop through an example. Those with insight into such things know how fortunate it is for later life when, during childhood, they heard about a respected relative they had not yet seen. Then, one day, they had the opportunity to visit that person. They went to visit that relative with a shyness and with everything that was contained in the picture developed within them. They stood there shyly as the door was opened. That first encounter with a highly respected person is certainly memorable. To have had the opportunity to respect someone in that way is something that takes deep root in the human soul, and it can still bear fruit in later life.

It is the same with all truly living concepts taught to children and not simply stuffed into them. If you can get a child to look up with true respect to you as a teacher, as an accepted authority, you then create something for the child's later life. We could describe it as follows. We know that there are people who, when they have reached a certain age, spread goodness in their environment. They do not need to say much, but their words act as a kind of blessing; it is contained in their voice, not in the content of their words. It is certainly a blessing for people when, during their childhood, they met such people. If we look back on the life of such a person of fifty or sixty and see what occurred during childhood between the change of teeth and puberty, if we look at what that person learned, we realize that person learned respect, a respect for morality. We realize that such a person learned to look up to things properly, to look up to the higher forces in the world. We might say that such a person learned how to pray properly. When someone learns to pray in the right way, the respect they learn is transformed into powers of blessing in old age, powers that act like a good deed for others in their presence. To express it pictorially, someone who never learned to fold their hands in prayer as a child will never develop the strength later in life to spread their hands in blessing.

It is important that we do not simply stuff abstract ideas into children, but that we know how to proceed with children when we want to create within their souls something fruitful for all of life. Therefore, we do not abstractly teach children to read and write, but begin artistically with writing and allow all the abstraction within letters to arise from pictures. In that way, we teach children to write in a way appropriate to the child's needs. We do not simply appeal to the child's capacity to observe, to the head alone, but to the entire human being. First, we teach children to write. When the child has learned to write in this way—so that the child's entire being, and not simply the head, participates in the picture—then what we give the child is appropriate. After children learn to write, they can learn to read.

Anyone caught up in today's school system might say that such children would learn to read and write more slowly than otherwise. However, it is important that the tempo of learning is proper. Basically, children should learn to read only after the age of eight, so that we can develop reading and writing pictorially and artistically.

Those who have genuine knowledge of human beings through true vision of soul and spirit can observe subtle details and then bring those observations into teaching. Suppose we have a child who walks too heavily. That comes about because the child's soul was improperly affected before the change of teeth. We can improve the situation by enlivening what previously formed the child by teaching through artistically presented pictures. Thus, someone who truly understands the human being will teach a child who walks too heavily about painting and drawing. By contrast, a child whose step is too light, too dancing, should be guided more toward music. That has a tremendous moral effect on the child's later character development.

Thus, in each case, if we can truly see the human being, we will understand what we need to bring into our pictures.

Until the change of teeth the child's closest and most appropriate place is within the circle of the family and the parents. Nursery school and play groups follow. We can appropriately develop games and activities when we understand how they affect the child's physical organism. We need only imagine what happens when a child receives a store-bought doll, a "beautiful" doll with a beautifully painted face. We can see that such a child develops thick blood (these things are not visible in the normal anatomy) and that this disturbs the child's physical body. We simply do not realize how much we sin in that way, how it affects the child. If we make for the child a doll from a few rags, and if this is done with the child—simply painting the eyes on the rags so that the child sees this and sees how we create the doll—then the child will take that activity into its body. It enters into the child's blood and respiratory system.

Suppose we have a melancholic girl. Anyone who looks at such a child externally, without any view of the soul, would simply say, "Oh, a melancholic child; inwardly dark. We need to put very bright colors around her and make toys red and yellow for her wherever possible. We must dress the child brightly, so that she awakens in bright colors, so that she will be awakened." No, she won't! That would only be an inner shock for the child, and it would force all her life forces in the opposite direction. We should give a melancholic and withdrawn child blue or blue violet colors and toys. Otherwise, the bright colors would overstimulate such an inwardly active child. We can thus bring the child's organism into harmony with her surroundings and cure what is perhaps too flighty and nervous because of being surrounded by bright colors.

From a genuine understanding of the human being, we can gain an idea of what we should teach and do with children, right down to the finest details, and thus gain direct help for our work. You can see that this way of teaching might seem to support current ideas about what children should learn at a particular age—that we should stuff such things into them and about how we should occupy them. However, if you realize that children can take from their environment only what already exists within their bodies, then you might say the following. Suppose we have a child who does not tend to be robustly active, but always works in details—that is, tends to work rather artistically. If you insist that the child be very active outwardly, then just those tendencies within the child that are for detailed work will wither. The tendencies toward activity that you want to develop because you have deluded yourself into thinking that they are common to all humanity, that everyone should develop them, will also certainly wither. The child has no interest in that; the work assigned between the change of teeth and puberty is done, and nothing sticks, nothing grows within the child through forcing things. Throughout the kind of education we are discussing, it is always important that the teacher have a good sense of what lives within the child and can, from what is observed within the child's body, soul, and spirit, practice every moment what is right through the teacher's own instinct for teaching.

In this way, the teacher can see the pedagogy needed for the children. In the Waldorf school, we discover the curriculum in each child. We read from the children everything we are to do from year to year and month to month and week to week so that we can bring them what is appropriate and what their inner natures require. The teaching profession demands a tremendous amount of selflessness, and because of this it cannot in any way accept a preconceived program. We need to direct our teaching entirely toward working with the children so that the teacher, through the relationship to the children developed by standing alongside them, provides nothing but an opportunity for the children to develop themselves.

You can best accomplish this between the ages of seven and fourteen—that is, during elementary school—by refraining completely from appealing to the intellect, focusing instead on the artistic. Then, you can develop through pictures what the body, soul, and spirit need. Therefore, we should present morality as pictures when the child is about nine or ten years old. We should not provide moral commandments; we should not say that this or that is good or evil. Instead, we should present good people to the children so that they can acquire sympathy for what is good, or perhaps, present the children with evil people so that they can acquire antipathy toward what is evil. Through pictures we can awaken a feeling for the nature of morality.

All of those things are, of course, only suggestions that I wanted to present concerning the second stage of childhood. In the third part of my lecture today, I want to show how we can bring it all together as a foundation for education—not merely education for a particular time in childhood, but for all of human life. We will continue with that after the second part has been translated.

(George Adams delivered the second part of the lecture.)

We can best see how this way of educating can achieve the proper effects for all of human life if we look specifically at eurythmy in education. The eurythmy we have performed publicly in London during the past days has a pedagogical side, also.

Eurythmy is an art in which people or groups of people express the movements in the depths of human nature. Everything expressed in those movements arises systematically from the activity within the human organism, just as human speech or song does. In eurythmy, no gesture or movement is haphazard.

What we have is a kind of visible speech. We can express anything we can sing or speak just as well through the visible movements of eurythmy. The capacity of the entire human being for movement is repressed in speech, it undergoes a metamorphosis in the audible tones and is formed as visible speech in eurythmy.

We have brought eurythmy into the Waldorf school for the lowest grades all the way to the highest. The children, in fact, enter into this visible speech just as the soul makes a corresponding expression for the sounds of audible speech. Every movement of the fingers or hands, every movement of the entire body is thus a sound of speech made visible. We have seen that children between the change of teeth and puberty live just as naturally into this form of speech as a young child lives into normal audible speech. We have seen that the children's entire organism—that is, body, soul, and spirit (since eurythmy is also a spirit and soul exercise) find their way just as naturally into eurythmy speech as they do into oral speech. Children feel they have been given something consistent with their whole organism. Thus, along with gymnastics derived from an observation of the physical body, we have eurythmy arising from an observation of the child's spirit and soul. Children feel fulfilled in eurythmy movements, not only in their physical body or in an ensouled body, but in a spiritually permeated soul within a body formed by that soul. To say it differently, what people experience through eurythmy acts in a tremendously living manner on everything living within them as tendencies and, on the other side, has just as fruitful an effect on all of life.

Regardless of how well children do in gymnastics, if they perform these exercises only according to the laws of the physical body, these exercises will not protect the children from all kinds of metabolic illnesses later in life. For instance, you cannot protect them from illnesses such as rheumatism, which may cause metabolic illnesses later. What you gain through gymnastics results in a kind of thickening of the physical body. However, what you can effect by developing movements that arise from the spirit and soul makes the spirit and soul ruler of the bodies of the soul and physical for all of life. You cannot keep a sixty-year-old body from becoming fragile through gymnastics. If you educate a child properly, however, so that the child's movements in gymnastics arise from the soul, you can keep the child's body from becoming fragile in later life. You can inhibit such things if you teach pictorially during elementary school so that the picture that would otherwise occupy the soul can move into the body.

Thus, this pictorial language, eurythmy, is nothing but gymnastics permeated with soul and spirit. You can see that gymnastics permeated by soul and spirit is directed only toward a balanced development of the child's body, soul, and spirit; and you can see that what can be ingrained during childhood can be fruitful throughout life. We can do that only when we feel like gardeners tending plants. The gardener will not, for example, artificially affect the plant's sap flow, but will provide from outside only opportunities for the plant to develop itself. A gardener has a kind of natural reluctance to artificially alter plant growth. We must also have a respectfulness about what children need to develop within their own lives. We will, therefore, always be careful not to teach children in an unbalanced way. The principle of authority I discussed before must live deeply within the child's soul. Children must have the possibility of learning things they cannot yet intellectually comprehend, but learn anyway because they love the teacher. Thus, we do not take away from children the possibility of experiencing things later in life.

If I have already comprehended everything as a child, then I could never have the following kind of experience. Suppose something happens to me around age thirty-five that reminds me of something I learned from a beloved teacher or a loved authority, something I had learned from that authority through my desire to believe. However, now I am more mature and slowly a new understanding arises within me. Returning in maturity to things we learned earlier, but did not fully comprehend, has an enlivening effect. It gives an inner satisfaction and strengthens the will. We cannot take that away from children if we respect their freedom and if we want to educate them as free human beings. The foundation of the educational principle I am referring to is the desire to educate people as free beings. That is why we should not develop the child's will through intellectual moral reasoning. We need to be clear that when we develop moral views in the child's feeling between the ages of seven and fourteen, the child can, after maturing and moving into life, then comprehend intellectual and moral feelings and the will. What permeates the will, and what arises out of the will from the esthetic feeling developed earlier, enlivens morality and, insofar as it arises from freedom, gives people strength and inner certitude.

You see, if you want to use the kind of education we are discussing properly, you will not simply look at childhood, but will also look at people later in life. You will want what you give to children to act just as the natural growth and development of the plant acts to produce a flower that blooms. If we want a blossoming, we do not dare to want the plant to develop too quickly. Instead, we await the slow development from the root to the stem to the leaf to the flower and, finally, to the fruit, unfolding and developing freely in the sunlight. That is the picture we need to keep before us as the goal of education. Our desire is to nurture the root of life in children. However, we want to develop this root so that life slowly and flexibly forms physically, soulfully, and spiritually from our care during childhood. We can be certain that, if we respect human freedom, our teaching will place people in the world as free beings. We can be certain that the root of education can develop freely if we do not enslave children to a dogmatic curriculum. Later in life, under the most varied circumstances, children can develop appropriately as free human beings.

Of course, this kind of education puts tremendous demands on the teacher. However, do we dare presume that the most complete being here on Earth—the human being—can be taught at all if we do not penetrate fully the characteristics of that being? Shouldn't we believe—concerning human beings and what we do with them—that they hold a place of honor, and that much of what we do is a kind of religious service? We must believe that. We must be aware that education demands of us the greatest level of selflessness. We must be able to forget ourselves completely and plunge into the nature of the child in order to see what will blossom in the world as an adult human being. Selflessness and a true desire to deepen your understanding of human nature, and gaining a true understanding of humanity—these are the basic elements of genuine teaching.

Why shouldn't we recognize the necessity of devotion to such teaching, since we must certainly admit that teaching is the most noble activity of human life? Teaching is the most noble thing in all human life on the Earth.

That is progress. The progress we achieve through teaching is this: the younger generations, given to us from the divine worlds, develop through what we, the older generations, have developed in ourselves; and these younger generations move a step beyond us in human progress. Isn't it obvious to every right-thinking person that, in bringing such service to humanity—that is, in bringing the best and most beautiful things of previous generations as an offering to the younger generations—we teach in the most beautiful and humane way?

(*George Adams concluded the English translation.*)

3

Education and Art

STUTTGART — MARCH 25, 1923

Ladies and Gentlemen! From the time of Ancient Greece, a familiar and much discussed phrase has come to us like a warning cry to the depths of the human soul: "Human Being, know yourself!" These words, though rarely heeded as such, call us with power. They can be interpreted as asking us to become aware, not only of our true being in the most important activities of soul and spirit, but also of our significance as human beings in the world order.

Ordinarily, when such a call sounds forth from a culturally significant center at a particular time in history, it does not indicate something easily attainable, but rather to the lack of ability; it points toward something not easily fulfilled.

If we look back at earlier historical epochs, not superficially or theoretically but with a real feeling for history, we shall experience how such a call indicates a decrease rather than an increase in the power of human self-knowledge. In previous times of human evolution, religious experience, artistic sense, and the inner comprehension of ideals still worked together in harmony. One can feel how, at that time when religion, art, and science still formed a unity, human beings felt themselves, naturally, to be likenesses or images of the divine spirit, living within and permeating the world. They felt themselves to be God-sent entities on Earth. During those ancient days, it was self-evident that seeking knowledge of the human being was also part of seeking knowledge of the gods—divine knowledge—the spiritual foundations, experienced and thought of as the ground of the world, and felt to be working also in the human being.

In remote times, when human beings spoke the word that would represent the word *I* in our current language, it expressed for them both the essence of fundamental world forces and their inherent world-being. The word thus indicated that the human self resonated with something much greater than the individual self, something pointing at the creative working in the universe. During the course of evolution, it became more and more difficult to reach what had been accepted naturally at one time, just as perceptible as color is today to our eyes. If these earlier people had heard the call for self-knowledge (which could hardly have come from an earthly being), if they had perceived the call "Know yourself!" as coming from a supersensible being, they may well have answered, "Why is it necessary to make such an effort for self-knowledge?" For human beings saw and felt themselves as reflections of the divine spirit that shines, sounds, warms, and blesses throughout the world. They felt that if one knows what the wind carries through the trees, what the lightning sends through the air, what rolls in the thunder, what constantly changes in the cloud formations, what lives in a blade of grass, what blossoms in the flower, then one also knows the human self.

A time came when such knowledge of the world, which was simultaneously knowledge of the divine spirit, was no longer possible, due to humanity's increasing spiritual independence; the phrase "Know yourself!" began to be heard in the depths of human consciousness. It indicated something that had been a natural gift until that point, but was now becoming an exertion.

There is an important epoch of human evolution between the earlier admonition "Know yourself!" and another phrase coined much later, in our own times, in the last third of the nineteenth century. The later saying, voiced by the eminent natural scientist Du Bois-Reymond, rang out like a negative answer to the Apollonian call "Know yourself!" with the word *Ignorabimus*—"we are fated to ignorance."[1] *Ignorabimus* expressed Du Bois-Reymond's opinion that modern knowledge of nature, despite its immense progress, was fated to be arrested at the frontier of natural science. A significant stretch of human soul development exists between these two historically momentous utterances. In the meantime, enough inner human strength survived as a residue of ancient times that, what previously had been a matter of course—that is, to look for the essence of the human being in the outer appearance of divine existence—now meant that, in due time, by strength of inner effort, the human being would gradually attain self-knowledge again. But this force of self-knowledge became increasingly weaker. By the last third of the nineteenth century, it had become so weak that, after the sun of self-knowledge had set, the negative counterpart of the Apollonian positive was heard: "Human being, you will never know yourself."

For contemporary natural history, attuned to the needs of our time, to confess it impossible to fathom the secrets of consciousness working in matter, amounts to admitting that knowledge of the human being is completely unattainable. At this point something else must be mentioned: When the call "Human Being, know yourself!" was heard, self-knowledge, which in earlier times had also been knowledge of God, was

---

1. Emil Heinrich Du Bois-Reymond (1818–1896), German physiologist and professor in Berlin. Investigated animal "electricity," muscle and nerve physiology, and metabolism.

already passing through its twilight stages; and in just that way the renunciation of self-knowledge was in its twilight stages by the time we were told, "Resign yourself! There is no self-knowledge, no knowledge of the human being."

Again the words indicate not so much what is said directly, as to its opposite, which is what present-day humanity is experiencing. Precisely because the power of self-knowledge has increasingly weakened, the urge for the knowledge of the human being has made itself felt, an urge that comes, not from the intellect, nor from any theoretical ideas, but from the realm of the heart, from the deepest recesses of the soul. It was felt generally that the methods of natural science could not discover humankind's true nature, despite the brilliant successes of natural-scientific research that had benefited humanity to such a degree. At the same time there was a strong feeling that, somehow, paths must exist.

The birth of this new search for knowledge of the human being, as expressed by natural scientists, included, side by side with other fundamental branches of life, the pedagogical movement, the movement to evolve a proper relationship between the human being and the growing human being—between the adult and the child who needs to be educated and taught. This movement prompted the call most strongly for a renewal of knowledge of the human being, even if outwardly expressed in opposite terms—namely, that such knowledge was beyond human reach. At the very time that these sentiments were being expressed, there was a growing conviction among those who really cared for the education of the young, that intellectualism, knowledge based only on external sense observation and its consequent interpretation, was unsuitable to provide human beings with what they need to teach and educate young people, the growing young men and women. One therefore heard increasingly the call for changing priorities between the training of rational thinking, which has made such precious contributions to the modern world, and the education of the children's feeling life and of the forces of human will. Children were not to be turned into "know-it-alls," but overall capacities for practical life were to be nurtured and encouraged.

There is one strange omission in this general demand for a renewal of education, however: the necessity to base educational demands on a clear insight into the evolving human being, into the child, rather than to depend on the teachers' vague subconscious instincts. The opinion is that, while nature can be known, it is impossible to penetrate human nature in depth and in full consciousness in a way that would help educators. Indeed, one particular trend of modern pedagogy renounces any attempt to develop a conscious, thoughtful understanding of the human being, depending instead on the teachers' supposed educational instincts. Any unbiased judge of the current situation has to acknowledge the existence (among a wide range of very praiseworthy pedagogical movements) of a strong tendency to build educational aims on elementary and instinctual human nature. One depends on vague, instinctive impulses because of a conviction that it is impossible to gain conscious knowledge of the depths of the human being.

Only when one can see through such an attitude in the contemporary spiritual and cultural life with the human interest it deserves, can one appreciate the aims of the science of the spirit as it applies to the development of pedagogical sense and competence. This science of the spirit does not draw its substance from ancient forms of human knowledge; nevertheless, it offers new possibilities in the praiseworthy natural-scientific urge to penetrate into the depths of human nature, especially in the field of education. Knowledge of the human being can only be attained in full consciousness, for we have definitely passed the stage when human beings lived by instinct. We cannot, of

course, jettison instinct or elemental-primeval forces altogether, yet we need to work toward a fully conscious penetration into all the beings that come to meet us in human life.

It may feel nice to hear that we should not depend too much
on intellect and reason, and thus we should trust again in the
mysterious working of instinctive impulses. But this nice feeling is inappropriate for the current time, because, due to our
being human and thus caught in human evolution, we have
lost the old certainty of instinctual experience. We need to conquer a new certainty that will be no less primeval and no less
elementary than earlier forms of experience, one capable of
allowing us to plunge into the sphere of consciousness.

The very people who rush enthusiastically toward knowledge using the approach and methods that are used quite justi-
fiably today to explore nature, will also come to realize that this
particular way of using the senses, this way of using instruments in the service of experimental research cannot lead to
knowledge of the human being; nor will we find it in a certain
way of making rational judgments about sensory knowledge, a
particular way of investigating nature. The natural scientists
themselves will have to concede that a knowledge of the human
being must exist that flows from completely different sources
than the ones we tap these days in an attempt to invade the
being of external reality.

In my books *How to Know Higher Worlds* and *An Outline of
Occult Science*, I have described the forces that the human being
must extract from the depths of the self.[2] I have shown that it is
possible to awaken forces in the human soul so that one can recognize something purely spiritual behind outer appearances,
and that, by allowing dormant forces to reveal themselves, one
can recognize spirit working in, and permeating, all matter.

---

2. See the reading list at the back of the book.

Two things must be understood fully about spiritual science: First, it is impossible to fathom the secrets of human nature by knowledge gained exclusively from natural science; second, it is possible to penetrate the spiritual world in the same fully conscious state that so-called empirical research uses in the sense world, and with the same clarity. However, I must quickly add that the importance of what has just been said can be appreciated and confirmed only through personal, practical experience in matters of spiritual knowledge.

People who try—and this has been done again and again—to apply the methods of experimental laboratory research to the investigation of the human being will not succeed, for the essence of human nature must be experienced in one's own self to be experienced at all in a living way. It is well known that, in the absence of self-knowledge, one remains always at the periphery of the human being, and I would like to make the following paradoxical statement: If a researcher were to apply the natural-scientific research method to the study of the human being, and then to verify the findings, applied them to his or her own being, believing this to really be what true humanity is about, the following would happen. Precisely when such a person felt most enthusiastic, the following realization would jump up in front of the soul: When I experience myself through the natural-scientific method, applying all my senses and all my powers of knowledge, I still feel the way one would feel looking at one's own skeleton. The experience of such natural-scientific investigation would in fact be devastating. Human beings would "skeletize" themselves. To experience this feeling is to touch on the impulse that gave rise to spiritual science. We must bring the essence of the human being out in ways other than through bringing forth lifeless nature.

What kind of human knowledge will lead to this goal? It certainly cannot be the kind that makes us feel as if in our soul and spirit we were mere skeletons; there must be a way of evoking different images. Let us look at our blood circulation and our breathing. Although we are not generally aware of them in any great detail, they form an essential part of our life. The way we normally experience our blood circulation and our breathing when in good health represents a wholeness, even without our being able to put this perception into so many words. We experience it simply as part of our feeling healthy. Something similar must surely exist with regard to our knowledge of the human being. It must be possible to form ideas and perceptions of the human being that can be worked through inwardly, so that one experiences them as a natural part of the human entity, comparable with experiencing one's breathing and blood circulation as a natural part of health. But then the question arises: What will lead us to an understanding of the child's nature, with which we, as educators and teachers, must work?

How do we learn to know external sensory nature? Through our senses. Through our eye we gain knowledge of the multiple world of light and color. In order to make any of the world phenomenon part of our soul content, we must have the appropriate sense experiences, and we need the relevant sense organs for what is to become part of our soul content. If we study the wonderful construction of the human eye and the way it is linked to the brain, we will experience deeply what Goethe felt when he repeated the verse of an ancient mystic:

> Were not the eye alike the Sun,
> How could we ever see the light?
> Lived not in us God's own great power,
> How could the Divine ever bring delight?

This Sun-like element of the eye, working selflessly within the inner human being, enables us to receive the external light.

We must look at the sense organs themselves if we want to understand the human connection with the external world, or if we wish to make any soul experience our own. Now let us look at the specific organ that can lead us to a true knowledge of the human being. Which sense organ would lead us to such a knowledge? We get to know external nature through our eyes, our ears and the other senses. For knowledge of the spiritual world, it is the spiritually enlightened being, which can be attained by following the paths described in *How to Know Higher Worlds*. In that book I describe two polarities in human striving for knowledge: On the one side is the knowledge resulting from what the physical senses give us; on the other side is the knowledge of the spirit, which pervades and weaves through both outer nature and the inner realm of the human being. This spiritual knowledge can be gained whenever human beings make themselves into spiritual sense organs by somehow transmuting all the forces of their human nature.

The field of knowledge of the human being lies precisely between these two poles. If we restrict ourselves to knowing external nature as transmitted to us through the senses, we cannot reach the essence of the human being for the reasons already stated. If we are cognizant of the spiritual aspects only, we have to transport ourselves to such heights of soul and spirit that the immediacy of the human being standing before us in the world vanishes. (You can read about this aspect in *Occult Science* and in my other writings dealing with the spiritual science I am speaking of here.) We need something that gives us even more intimate access to the human being than the subtle sense allowing us to see human beings as a part of the spirit nature that permeates the whole world. Just as I need the eye to perceive color, so a particular sense is needed for unmediated perception of the human being. What could such a sense be like at the present stage of human evolution? How can we penetrate the nature of human beings as they exist in the world, in the same way that we can penetrate the multiplicity of colors through the wonderful organization of the eye or the multiplicity of sounds through that of the ear? Where do we find this sense for the perception of the human essence?

It is none other than the sense granted us for the appreciation of art; the artistic sense can transmit to us spirit shining in matter, and revealed as the beauty we appreciate in art. At the present stage of evolution, this artistic sense allows us to apprehend the essence of what is truly human so that it can enter practical spheres of life. I know very well how paradoxical such a statement must sound to the ears of our contemporaries. But if I have the courage to think, to their very end, the concepts and ideas by which we comprehend external nature, and if having felt my way into them with all my humanity, I can say to myself that my ideas, my concepts have really brought me very close to nature, then I will feel that something at that very boundary is pulling me free of the limitations of these concepts and ideas, allowing me to soar up toward an artistic formulation of them.

This was why in 1894 I wrote the following words in the introduction to *The Philosophy of Spiritual Activity*: "To fully understand the human being, an artistic appreciation of ideas is needed, not merely an abstract comprehension of ideas."[3] A real enlivening is required to make the leap that transforms the abstraction of concepts we use to understand nature into artistic display. This is possible. It requires that knowledge be allowed to flow into art, which leads to the development of the artistic sense. As long as we remain within the boundaries of natural science, we have to acknowledge that we will never understand how consciousness is connected with matter; but

---

3. The original preface is included in *The Philosophy of Spiritual Activity: A Philosophy of Freedom*, Rudolf Steiner Press, London, 1992.

the moment we allow anything to flow naturally from the realm of ideas into an artistic view, the scales fall from our eyes. Everything in the realm of idea and concept is transformed into an artistic seeing, and what we see in this way spreads over the essence of humanity, just as the colors conceived by the eye spread their hues over the outer appearance of plants or other natural phenomena. Just as the physical organ of the eye, in the process of conceiving color, merges with the essence of color phenomena in nature, so the artistic sense grows inwardly in conjunction with the nature of the human being as a whole. We need to have seen colors with our eyes before we can think them. Likewise, only after we have had a vision of the nature of the human being through this artistic sense, can our abstract concepts and ideas fully encompass it.

If science thus becomes an art, then all our knowledge of the human being, and all our deliberations about first forming an artistic picture of the human being, will not turn to a bag of bones in the soul; instead, we will be at one with our own concepts and artistic ideas about the human being, and they will flow into and through the soul just as blood and breath circulate through the body. Something will reside in us that is as full of life as our sensations are when our breathing and blood circulation function normally and give us a sense of health and well being.

A sense of wholeness then embraces the entire nature of the human being, similar to a general feeling of health with regard to our physical organization; this sense will include something that is possible only when the artistic sense has attained the intimate contemplation of the human being living here in the present, not the elevated human being of insufficiently grounded spiritual speculation.

If we consider what such knowledge will eventually yield— knowledge that, like our breathing and blood circulation, continuously and in each of its aspects becomes will and activity—

we will find that this extended metaphor helps us even further; for it is more than a mere comparison, and it has not been picked out in the abstract, but grows out of reality itself. What is it that causes our feeling of health, emanating from our entire constitution? What happens in such a general feeling of health, which, by the way, can be a very subtle feeling? It is the recognition that I, the human being, am so organized that I can look at myself as a healthy person standing in the world. What does it mean to be a healthy human being?

The crown of human life, the power of love is expressed in the healthy human being. Ultimately health and all healthy soul forces stream together into a feeling permeated with love, enabling me to acknowledge the person next to me, because I acknowledge the healthy human being in myself. Thus, out of this knowledge of the healthy human being sprouts love for our neighbor, whom we recognize as being like us. Our own self is found in another human being. Such knowledge of human nature does not become the theoretical instruction given to a technician who then applies it mechanically; rather, it becomes a direct inner experience leading immediately into practical life. For in its transformation it flows into the power of love and becomes an active form of human knowledge. If as teacher and educator, I meet a child through my knowledge of what a human being is, then an understanding of the child will blossom within my unfolding soul and spiritual love. I no longer need instructions based on the example of natural science and on theories about child development. All I need is to experience the knowledge of the human being, in the same way that I experience healthy breathing and healthy blood circulation as bases of my general health. Then the proper form of knowledge, correctly stimulated and enlivened, will become a pedagogical art.

What must this knowledge of the human being become? The answer will be found in what has been already said. We must be able to allow this knowledge of the human being to fly out on the wings of love over all our surroundings, and especially upon the children. Our knowledge of the human being must be transformed into an inner attitude where it is alive in the form of love. This is the most important basis for teaching today. Education must be seen as a matter of one's own inner attitude, not as a matter of thinking up various schemes, such as how to avoid training the child's intellect exclusively. We could constantly reiterate this tenet, of course, and then go about it in a thoroughly intellectual way, taking it for granted, for example, that teachers should use their intellects to think up ways to protect their pupils from intellectualism! It goes without saying that our work must begin with the teachers. We must encourage them not to fall back entirely on the intellect, which, by itself, never has an artistic nature. Starting with the teachers, we will create the proper conditions for the theory and practice of education, based on our knowledge of the human being and given in a form suitable for nurturing the child. This will establish the necessary contact between teacher and child, and it will turn our knowledge of the human being, through the working of love, into right education and training.

Natural science alone cannot understand how consciousness works in the physical organization. Why is this? Because it cannot comprehend how the artistic experience occurs and how it is formed. Knowledge of the human being makes us realize that consciousness is an artist whose material is the material substance of the human being. As long as knowledge of the human being is not sought with an artistic sense, the state of *ignorabimus* will hold sway. We must first begin to realize that human consciousness is an artist working creatively with matter itself; if we want to comprehend the true nature of the human being, we must acknowledge the artistic creator in each individual. Only then will we get beyond the stage of *ignorabimus*. At the same time, knowledge of the human being cannot be theoretical, but must able to enter the sphere of will. It will directly enter the practical sphere of life and feel at home there.

If the evolving child is viewed from this perspective, with insight stemming from an artistic sense and carried on wings of love, we will see and understand very much. I should like to describe just one example: Let us look at the extraordinary phase when the child undergoes the transition from playing to working. All children play. They do so naturally. Adults, on the other hand, have to work to live. They find themselves in a situation that demands it. If we look at social life today, we could characterize the difference between the child at play and the adult at work in the following way: Compared to the activities of the adult, which are dictated by necessity, the child's play is connected with an inner force of liberation, endowing the playing child with a feeling of well-being and happiness. You need only observe children at play. It is inconceivable that they are not in full inner accord with what they are doing. Why not? Because playing is a liberating experience to children, making them eager to release this activity from the organism. Freeing, joyful, and eager to be released—this is the character of the child's play.

What about the adult's work? Why does it often, if not usually, become an oppressive burden? (And this will be even more so in the future.) We could say that the child grows from an experience of liberation while playing into the experience of the oppressive burden of work, dictated to the adult by social conditions. Doesn't this great contrast beg us to ask: How can we build a bridge from the child's liberating play activity to the burdensome experience in the sphere of the adult workday?

If we follow the child's development with the artistic understanding I spoke of just now, we will find such a bridge in the role art plays at school. If applied properly as an educational tool, art will lead from the child's liberating play activity to the stage of adult work. With the help of art, this work no longer needs be an oppressive burden. Unless we can divest work of its oppressive character, we can never solve the social question. Unless the polarity between the young child's playing and the adult's burdensome daily work is balanced by the right education, the problem of labor will reappear again and again in different guises.

What does it mean to introduce the artistic element into education? One could easily form misconceptions about artistic activities, especially at school. Everyone agrees that it is essential to train the child's intellect. This notion has become so deeply ingrained in modern consciousness that indifference toward training the intellect is very unlikely to spread. Everyone can see also that, without moral education, one cannot do justice to human dignity, and the human being cannot be considered fully developed. In general, there is still a certain feeling that an immoral person is not fully human, but is disabled, at least in regard to the human soul and spirit. And so, on the one hand people assume that the intellect must be trained, and, on the other, that genuine human dignity must also be cultivated at school, including the concepts of a sacred sense of duty and human virtues. But the same attention is not given to what the human being can be presented with in full freedom and love— that is, the artistic element.

The high esteem for what is human and an extraordinary love for the human being are needed during one's evolving childhood days; this was the case for Schiller, whose (alas!) insufficiently known *Letters on the Esthetic Education of the Human Being* was based on those qualities.[4] We find in them a

---

4. Johann Christoph Friedrich von Schiller (1759–1805), German poet, playwright, and critic.

genuine appreciation of the artistic element in education, rooted in German culture. We can begin with these letters, and spiritual science will deepen our understanding. Look, for example, at child's play and how it flows forth simply because it is in a child's nature to be active. See how children liberate from their organization something that takes the form of play; their humanity consists of something that takes the form of play. Observe how necessity forces us to perform work that does not flow directly from the wholeness of our human nature; it can never express all of our nature. This is how we can begin to understand human development from childhood to adulthood.

There is one thing, however, that we should never lose sight of; usually, when observing children at play, people do so from the perspective of an adult. If this were not so, one would not hear again and again the trifling exhortation that "children should learn through play." The worst thing you could do is teach children that work is mere play, because when they grow up, they then will look at life as if it were only a game. Anyone who holds such a view must have observed children at play only with an adult's eyes, believing that children bring the same attitude to play as adults do. Play is fun for an adult, an enjoyment, a pleasure, the spice of life. But for children, play is the very stuff of life. Children are absolutely earnest about play, and the very seriousness of their play is a salient feature of this activity. Only by realizing the earnest nature of child's play can we understand this activity properly. And by watching how, in play, human nature pours itself in complete seriousness into the treatment of external objects, we can direct the child's inborn energy, capacity and gift for play into artistic channels. These still permit a freedom of inner activity while at the same time forcing children to struggle with outer materials, as we have to do in adult work. Then we can see how precisely this artistic activity makes it possible to conduct education so that the joy of engaging in artistic activities can be combined with the seriousness of play, contributing in this way to the child's character.

Particularly after the child enters school, until the ninth or tenth year, one may be in a position to use the artistic element, and this must be more than dallying in fairy tales; rather, whatever subject is being taught, the child's inherent impulse to play, which is such an intrinsic part of its makeup, can be guided into artistic activities. And when children enter the first or second grade, they are perfectly able to make this transition. However clumsy children of six or seven may be when modeling, painting, or finding their way into music and poetry, if teachers know how to permeate their lessons with artistry, even small children, as miniature sculptors or painters, can begin to have the experience that human nature does not end at the fingertips, that is, at the periphery of the skin, but flows out into the world. The adult human being is growing in children whenever they put their being into handling clay, wood, or paints. In these very interactions with the materials, children grow, learning to perceive how closely the human being is interwoven with the fabric of the world. And when working with musical sounds and colors, or handling wood, children grow outward into the world. If children are introduced to these artistic activities properly—however clumsy their first efforts may appear—they will greatly benefit from what is received in this way from the world. When music and poetry are brought to children, they experience the musical and poetical element in their own being. Then it is as if a heavenly gift had been bestowed on young students, enabling them to experience a second being within. Through sounds of music and poetry, it is as if a grace-filled being were sinking down into us through sounds of music and poetry, making us aware even in childhood, that in each of us something lives, which has come from spiritual heights to take hold of our narrow human nature.

If one lives this way with children, with the eye and mind of an artist and teaching them with a sensitive and artistic touch, their responses will reveal qualities that the teacher must endeavor to cultivate, however clumsy the children's first efforts may be when working with color, sound, or other artistic media. One learns to know children intimately, both their gifts and limitations; watching the artistic element of the sculpture as it flows from little hands, living in empathy with the child, one learns to recognize the strength with which the child directs every bit of attention and forces toward the spirit worlds, and then brings that back into the physical world of the senses. One learns to know the children's entire relationship to a higher spiritual world. And if music and poetry are brought to the children, as a teacher, one gains a glimpse of the latent strength in them, ready to develop later in life.

Having brought the children into close contact with the plastic, poetic, and musical arts, and having brought eurythmic movements into their bodies, having awakened to life through eurythmy what would otherwise be the abstract element of language, we create in the human being an inner harmony between the spirit-winged musical and poetic elements, and the spirit-permeated material elements of modeling and painting. Human consciousness, spiritually illumined, weaves soulfully and artistically into the physical corporeal part of the human being. One learns to teach by awakening spirit and soul in children, in such a way that teaching becomes health-permeating, stimulating growth and strength for all of life. This brings to mind a beautiful and deeply meaningful Greek expression. The ancient Greeks spoke of Phidias's statue of Zeus as "healing magic." Genuine art will not only take hold of soul and spirit, but it will also enhance health and growth. Genuine art has always had healing powers.

Educators and teachers who have the proper love for art and the necessary respect for human nature will always be in a position to implant the artistic element as a magic healing into all their teaching. Then training the intellect, which is a necessary part of schooling, as well as religious teaching and training the heart forces, will be permeated by an element that is inextricably connected to human freedom and human love. If teachers themselves feel a strong bond with the artistic element and appeal to the artistic appreciation in their pupils, and if they create an artistic atmosphere in the classroom, the proper teaching methods and human influence will stream out into all other aspects of education. Then they will not "save" the artistic element for other subjects, but let it flow and permeate all their teaching. The attitude must not be: Here are the main subjects—this one will train the intellect, this one the feelings and the sense of duty, and over there, separate, more or less on a voluntary basis, is the art lesson. On the contrary, art is in its proper place only when all teaching is arranged so that, at the right moment, the students' souls feel a need for the artistic; and art itself must be cultivated so that, in the artistic activities themselves, students feel the need for a rational understanding of, and dutiful concentration on, the things they have come to see as beautiful, as truly free, and thus as human. This is intended to indicate how art can pervade the entire field of education, how it can illumine and warm through the entire pedagogical and sermonizing realm of education. Art and the esthetic sense place knowledge of the human being at the meeting of purely spiritual knowledge on the one side, and external sensory knowledge on the other. It also helps lead us most beautifully into the practical aspects of education.

Through an art of teaching such as I have outlined, those who love art and respect humanity will assign art the proper place in the life of a school. They will do so from a feeling for human nature, condensed into a pedagogical attitude and a pedagogical life through daily contact with the students. They will not neglect the spiritual aspects nor those more connected with the physical world. If art occupies the proper place in school life it will also stimulate the correct approach to the students' physical training, since wherever art is applied in life, it opens a person to the spiritual light necessary for inner development. By its very nature, art can become permeated with the light of the spirit, and when this has happened it retains this light. Then, wherever art radiates, it permeates whatever it touches with the light it received from the spiritual Sun. It also permeates matter with light so that, outwardly radiant and shining with the light of soul, it can express spirit. Art can collect in itself the light of the universe. It can also permeate all earthly and material substance with shining light. This is why art can carry secrets of the spiritual world into the school and give children the light of soul and spirit; the latter will allow children to enter life so that they do not need to experience work as just a negative and oppressive burden, and, in our social life, therefore, work may gradually divest its burdensome load. By bringing art into school properly, social life can become enriched and freed at the same time, although that may sound unbelievable.

I will address other aspects tomorrow, when I speak of the place of morality and ethical attitudes in education. Today I only want to show that the spirit needed in schools can be magically engendered through art. If done properly, this light-filled art can produce a radiance in children that allows the soul to integrate into the physical body, and thus into the world, for the person's entire future life.

4

Education and the Moral Life

STUTTGART — MARCH 26, 1923

Everyone involved to any degree at all in social life will certainly feel that the moral aspect is one of the most important aspects in the entire field of education. At the same time, one realizes that it is precisely this aspect that is the most subtle and difficult one to handle, for it relates to the most intimate area of education.

I have already emphasized that educational practice needs to be built on real knowledge of, and insight into, the human being. The comprehension, perception and observation that I tried to characterize last night will give the knowledge necessary to train the child's cognitional capacities. Practically speaking, knowledge of the human being, supported by the science of the spirit, will enable one to reach, more or less easily, the child's powers of cognition. One will be able to find one's way to the child. If, on the other hand, one wishes to appeal to a child's artistic receptivity as described yesterday, which is equally important, it is necessary to find a way to each child individually, to have a sense for the way various children express themselves from an artistic comprehension of the world. When it comes to moral education, all of one's skill for sensitive observation and all of one's intimate psychological interest must be kept in mind, so that all the teacher's knowledge of the human being and of nature can be put at the service of what each child brings forth individually. To reach children in a moral way, the only choice is to approach each child on an individual basis. However, with regard to moral education, yet another difficulty has to be overcome—that is, an individual's sense of morality can only be appealed to through full inner freedom and with full inner cooperation.

This requires that educators approach moral teaching so that, when later in life the students have passed the age of formal education, they can feel free as individuals in every respect. What teachers must never do is to pass on to developing students the relics of their own brand of morality or anything derived from personal sympathies or antipathies in the moral realm. We must not be tempted to give our own ethical codes to young people as they make their way into life, since these will leave them unfree when it becomes necessary that they find their own moral impulses. We must respect and acknowledge the young person's complete inner freedom, particularly in the realm of moral education. Such respect and tolerance truly demand a great deal of selflessness from educators, and a renunciation of any self-interest. Nor is there, as is the case in all other subject matters, the opportunity of treating morality as a subject in its own right; as such, it would be very unfruitful. The moral element must be allowed to pervade all of one's teaching.

These difficulties can be overcome if we have truly made our own and imbued with spiritual science the knowledge that we bring to the pupils. Such knowledge, by opening one's eyes to each individual child, is all-important, particularly in this moral sphere. Ideally speaking, moral education would have to begin with the first breath taken in by the newborn, and in a certain sense, this really is what must be done. The great pedagogue Jean Paul (who is far too little recognized, unfortunately) said that a child learns more of value during the first three years of life than during the three years spent at university.[1] If these words were to be applied more to the moral aspect of education than to the cognitive and esthetic realms, they could be rephrased as follows: How an adult educator acts around the child is particularly important during the child's first years, until approximately the change of teeth—that is, until we receive the child into our schools.

The first life period really needs to be examined closely. Those who have embarked on the path to a true knowledge of the human being will need to consider three main stages during this first life period. At first sight, they do not seem directly connected with the moral aspect, but they nevertheless shed light on the child's entire moral life to come, right up to the point of death. In the first developmental phase of the child, the moral is tightly linked with the natural. In fact a crude psychology makes it difficult to notice the connection between later moral development and the child's natural development during these first years. The three stages in the child's development are usually not granted enough importance, yet they more or less determine the whole manner in which the child can become a human being inhabiting the Earth. The first one, when the child arises from what could be termed an animal-like existence yet in the human realm, is generally called "learning to walk." In learning to walk, the child has the possibility of placing into the world the entire system of movements—that is, the sum of all potential movements that human beings can perform with their limbs, so that a certain equilibrium is achieved. The second stage, when the child gains something for the entire course

1. Jean Paul Friedrich Richter (1763–1825), German writer of novels and romances; he also wrote on pedagogy (*Levana*, 1807) and art (*Vorschule der Ästhetic*, 1804).

of life, is "learning to speak." It is the force through which children integrate themselves into the human environment, whereas by learning to walk, children learned to integrate themselves into the whole world through a whole system of movements. All of this happens in the unconscious depths of the human soul. And the third element the child appropriates is "learning to think." However indistinct and childlike thinking may appear during the first life period, it is through learning to speak that the child gradually develops the capacity to make mental images, although in a primitive way at first.

We may ask: How does the child's acquisition of the three capacities of walking, speaking, and thinking lead to further development, until the conclusion of the first life period when the permanent teeth appear? The answer seems simple enough at first, but when comprehended with some depth, it sheds tremendous light on all of human nature. We find that during this first life period, ending with the change of teeth, the child is essentially a being who imitates in a state of complete unconsciousness, finds a relationship to the world through imitation and through trial and error. Until age seven, children are entirely given over to the influences coming from their environment. The following comparison can be made: I breathe in the oxygen of the air, which is part of my surroundings, to unite, at the next moment, my bodily nature with it, thus changing some part of the external world into my own inner world, where it works, lives, and weaves within me. Likewise, with each indrawn breath, children up to the age of seven bring outer influences into their "inner soul breath," by incorporating every gesture, facial expression, act, word, and even each thought coming from their surroundings. Just as the oxygen in my surroundings pulsates in my lungs, the instruments of my breathing, and blood circulation, so everything that is part of the surroundings pulsates through the young child.

This truth needs to stand before the soul's eye, not just superficially, but with real psychological impact. For remarkable consequences follow when one is sufficiently aware of the child's adaptation to its surroundings. I will discover how surprisingly the little child's soul reverberates with even an unspoken thought, which may have affected my facial expression only fleetingly and ever so slightly, and under whose influence I may have slowed or speeded up my movements, no matter how minutely. It is astonishing how the small details that remain hidden within the adult's soul are prolonged into the child's soul; how the child's life is drawn into the physical happenings of the surroundings, but also into the soul and spiritual environment. If we become sensitive to this fact of life, we will not permit ourselves even one impure, unchaste, or immoral thought near young children, because we know how imponderable influences work on children through their natural ability to imitate everything in their surroundings. A feeling for this fact and the attitude it creates are what make a person into a real educator.

Impressions that come from the company of adults around the child make a deep, though unconscious, imprint in the child's soul, like a seal in soft wax; most important among them are those images of a moral character. What is expressed as energy and courage for life in the child's father, how the father behaves in a variety of life situations, these things will always stamp themselves deeply into the child's soul, and will continue their existence there in an extraordinarily characteristic, though subtle and intimate, way. A father's energy will energize the entire organization of the child. A mother's benevolence, kindness, and love, surrounding the child like an invisible cocoon, will unconsciously permeate the child's inner being with a moral receptivity, with an openness and interest for ethical and moral matters.

It is very important to identify the origin of the forces in the child's organization. As unlikely and paradoxical as this may sound to modern ears, in the young child these forces derive predominately from the nerve-and-sense system. Because the child's ability to observe and perceive is unconscious, one does not notice how intensely and deeply the impressions coming from the surroundings enter its organization, not so much by way of various specific senses, as through the general "sensory being" of the child. It is generally known that the formation of the brain and of the nerves is completed by the change of teeth. During the first seven years the nerve-and-sense organization of the child could be compared with soft wax, in its plasticity. During this time, not only does the child receive the finest and most intimate impressions from the surroundings, but also, through the workings of energy in the nerve-and-sense system, everything received unconsciously radiates and flows into the blood circulation, into the firmness and reliability of the breathing process, into the growth of the tissues, into the formation of the muscles and skeleton. By means of the nerve-and-sense system, the child's body becomes like an imprint of the surroundings and, particularly, of the morality inherent in them. When we receive children into school at the time of the change of teeth, it is as if we received the imprint of a seal in the way the muscles and tissues are formed, even in the rhythm of breathing and blood circulation, in the rhythm of the digestive system with its reliability or its tendency toward sluggishness; in short, in the children's physical makeup we find the effects of the moral impressions received during the first seven years.

Today we have anthropology and we have psychology. Anthropology's main concern is the abstract observation of the physical aspect of the human being, while that of psychology is the abstract observation of the human soul and spirit as entities separate from the physical body. What is missing is the anthroposophical perspective, which observes the human being—body, soul, and spirit—as a unity; a point of view that shows everywhere how and where spirit is flowing into matter, sending its forces into material counterparts. The strange feature of our materialistic age is that materialism cannot recognize matter for what it is. Materialism believes it can observe matter wholly externally. But only if one can see how soul and spiritual processes are everywhere streaming and radiating their forces into material processes, does one really know what matter is. Through spiritual knowledge, one learns to know how matter works and what its real nature is. One could answer the question, "What is materialism?" by saying, "Materialism is the one worldview that does not understand matter."

This can be followed up even in details. If one has learned how to see the nature of the human being by viewing body, soul, and spirit as a unity, one will also recognize, in the formation of the muscles and tissues and in the breathing process, the ethical courage inherent in surroundings to which children have adapted during the first seven years. One sees, not only the moral love that warmed them, in the form of harmonious ethical attitudes in their environment, but also the consequences of disharmonious ethical attitudes and lack of love in the surroundings. Here a perceptive educator cannot help feeling that, by the time children are received by the school, they are already formed from the moral viewpoint—an insight that, taken seriously, could in itself engender a mood of tragedy. Given the difficult, disorderly, and chaotic social conditions of our time, it might almost seem preferable from a moral viewpoint if children could be taken into one's care soon after birth. For if one knows the human being out of a sensitive and refined psychology, one realizes how serious it is that by the time the child loses the first teeth, moral predispositions are fixed. On the other hand, this very same psychological insight offers the possibility of identifying the child's specific moral disposition and needs.

Children absorb environmental impressions, especially those of an ethical nature, as if in a dream. These dreams go on to affect the inmost physical organization of children. If children have unconsciously experienced and perceived courage, moral goodness, chastity, and a sense of truth, these qualities will live on in them. The presence of these qualities will be such that during the second life period, by the time children are in school, these qualities can still be mobilized.

I would like to illustrate this with an example: Let's assume that a child has spent the earliest years under the influence of an environment conducive to introversion. This could easily happen if a child witnesses lack of courage and even downright cowardice in the surroundings. If a child has seen in the environment a tendency to opt out of life, witnessed dissatisfaction with life or despondency, something in the child's inner being, so to speak, will evoke the impression of a continuously suppressed pallor. The educator who is not perceptive enough to observe such symptoms will find that the child takes in more and more intensely the effects of the lack of energy, the cowardice and doubt that has been witnessed in the surroundings. In some ways, even the child will exhibit such characteristics. But if one can view these things with greater depth, one will find that, what thus began as a distinct characterological disposition during the first seven years, can now be seized educationally and directed in a more positive way. It is possible to guide a child's innate timidity, lack of courage, shyness or fainthearted-ness so that these same inherent forces become transmuted into prudence and the ability to judge a situation properly; this pre-sumes that the teacher uses classroom opportunities to intro-duce examples of prudence and right judgment appropriate to the child's age and understanding.

Now let's assume that a child has witnessed in the surroundings repugnant scenes from which the child had inwardly recoiled in terror. The child will carry such experiences into school life in the form of a characterological disposition, affecting even the bodily organization. If such a trait is left unnoticed, it will continue to develop according to what the child had previously absorbed from the environment. On the other hand, if true insight into human nature shows how to reorient such negative characteristics, the latter can be transformed into a quality of purity and a noble feeling of modesty.

These specific examples illustrate that, although the child brings into school an imprint—even in the physical organization—of the moral attitudes witnessed in the earlier environment, the forces that the child has thus absorbed can be redirected in the most diverse ways.

In school we have an immensely important opportunity to correct an unbalanced disposition through a genuine, intimate, and practical sense of psychology, which can be developed by the educator who notices the various tendencies of character, will, and psyche in the students. By loving attentiveness to what the child's nature is revealing, the teacher is in a position to divert into positive channels what may have developed as an unhealthy or harmful influence from the early environment. For one can state explicitly that, in the majority of cases, nothing is ever so negative or evil in an ethical predisposition that the child cannot be changed for the better, given a teacher's insight and willing energy.

Contemporary society places far too little trust in the working of ethical and moral forces. People simply do not know how intensely moral forces affect the child's physical health, or that physical debilitation can be improved and corrected through proper and wholesome educational practice. But assuming we know, for example, that if left uncorrected a characteristic trait in a child could turn into violence later on, and that it can be changed so that the same child will grow into a courageous adult, quick and ready to respond to life's tasks—assuming that an intimate yet practical psychology has taught us these things, the following question will arise: How can we guide the moral education of the child, especially during the age of primary education? What means do we have at our disposal? To understand the answer, we will again have to look back at the three most significant stages in the development of the very young child.

The power of mental imagery and thinking that a child has developed until this point will continue to develop. One does not notice an abrupt change—perhaps at most, with the change of teeth, that the kind of mental imagery connected with memory takes on a different form. But one will notice that the soul and physical forces revealed in speech, which are closely linked to breathing and to the rhythmic system, will reappear, metamorphosed, during the years between the change of teeth and puberty. The first relationship to the realm of language is founded through the child's learning to speak during the first years of life. *Language* here includes not just language itself in the restricted meaning of the word, for the entire human being, body, soul, and spirit, lives in language. Language is a symptom of the entire threefold human being.

Approximately between the ages of seven and fourteen years, however, this relationship to language becomes prominent in the child in an entirely different—even reversed—way. At that point, everything related to the soul, outwardly expressed through the medium of language, will reach a different phase of development and take on a different character. It is true that these things happen mostly in the unconscious, but they are nevertheless instrumental for the child's entire development.

Between the ages of seven and fourteen, the child wrestles with what lives in the language, and if he or she should speak more than one language, in all the languages spoken. The child knows little of this struggle because it remains unconscious. The nature of this wrestling is due to increasingly intense merging of the sounds issuing from the rhythmic system with the pupil's thoughts, feelings, and will impulses. What is trying to evolve during this life period is the young adolescent's hold on the self by means of language.

It is extremely important, therefore, that we understand the fine nuances of character expressed in the ways students bring their speech and language into the classroom. The general directions I have already presented regarding the observation of the pupils' moral environment now sound back to us out of the tone of their voices, out of the very sound of their speech, if we are sensitive enough to perceive it. Through the way children use language, they present us with what I would call their *basic moral character.* Through the way we treat language and through the way students speak during lessons, every hour, even every minute, we are presented with the opportunity as teachers to guide what is thus revealed through speech, into the channels we consider appropriate and right. Very much can be done there, if one knows how to train during the age of primary education what, until the change of teeth, was struggling to become speech.

This is where we meet the actual principle of the growth and development that occurs during the elementary school age. During the first years up to the change of teeth, everything falls under the principle of imitation. At this stage the human being is an imitator. During the second life period, from the second dentition until puberty, the child is destined to surrender to what I would call *the authority of the teacher.* You will hardly expect me, the author of *Intuitive Thinking as a Spiritual Path,* to plead for the principle of authority per se. But for the time between the child's change of teeth and puberty, one has to plead for the principle of self-evident authority, simply because during these years the child's very nature needs to be able to look up to what comes from the authority of the adult.

The very young child observes the surroundings unconsciously. One could almost say that a child breathes in the whole character of the environment during the first seven years. The next seven years are spent not so much breathing in the environment, but listening to what it has to say. The word and its meaning now become the leading motive. The word becomes the guiding principle as a simple matter of human nature. During this stage the child learns to know about the world and the cosmos through the mediation of the educator. Whatever reaches the pupils through the mouth of the teacher as authority represents the truth to them. They observe beauty in gestures, in general conduct and again in the words spoken around them. Goodness is experienced through the sympathies and antipathies engendered by those in authority.

These few words give the main direction for moral education during the age between the second dentition and puberty. If we attempt to give the child abstract moral values upon its way, we will encounter inner resentment, not because of any inherent shortcomings in the child, but because of a natural response. On the other hand, if we can create moral pictures for the child, perhaps taken from the animal kingdom, letting animals appear symbolically in a moral light, and possibly extending this approach to include all of nature, then we can work for the good of the child, particularly during the seventh, eighth, and ninth years of life. If we create vivid, colorful human characters out of our own imagination and allow our own approval or disapproval of their deeds to shine through our descriptions, and if we allow our sympathies and antipathies to grow into definite feelings in the children that will lead them over into a more general moral judgment of good and evil, then our picture of the world cultivates age-appropriate moral judgements based in perceptions and feelings. But this particular way of presenting the world is of the essence. During the first years, the child has learned from direct perception. As we reach the primary school age, whatever comes toward the child, to strengthen a moral feeling leading to moral judgment, must have passed through the medium of those in authority. Now the teacher and educator must stand before the child as representatives of the order of the world. The child meets the teachers in order to receive the teachers' picture of the world, colored by their sympathies and antipathies. Through the feelings with which children meet the teachers, and through instinctual life, children themselves must find what is good and what is evil. The students have to receive the world through the mediation of the educator. The children are happy who, thanks to a teacher's interpretation of the world can form their own relationship to the world.

Those who have been fortunate enough to have enjoyed such a relationship with their teachers in childhood have gained something of value for the rest of their lives. People who say that children should learn intellectually and through their own observations, free from the influence of authority, speak like flagrant amateurs; for we do not teach children merely for the years during which they are under our care, but to benefit their whole lives. And the various life periods, right up to the point of death, are mutually interrelated in very interesting ways.

If, because of their teachers' natural authority, pupils have once accepted subject matter they could not yet fully comprehend with their powers of reasoning—for the intellectual grasp belongs to a later stage of development and works destructively if enforced too early—if they have accepted something purely out of love for their teachers, such content remains deeply preserved in their souls. At the age of thirty-five or forty perhaps, or possibly even later in life, it may happen that they speak of the following strange experience: Only now, after having lived through so many joys, pains, and disappointments, only now do I see the light of what I accepted at the age of eight out of my respect for my teacher's authority. This meaning now resurfaces, mingling with the many life experiences and the widening of horizons that have occurred meanwhile. What does such an experience mean for later life? A sensitive and empathetic psychology tells us that such events give off life-invigorating forces even into old age. Education gains new meaning from knowing that such an expansion of childhood experiences into older ages brings with it a new stimulus for life: we educate not only to satisfy the short-term needs of the child while at school, but also to satisfy the needs of life as a whole. The seeds laid into the child's soul must be allowed to grow with the child. Hence we must be aware that whatever we teach must be capable of further growth. Nothing is worse than our pedantic insistence that the child learn rigid, sharply outlined concepts. One could compare this approach with that of forcing the child's delicate hands into an iron glove to stop them from growing. We must not give the child fixed or finished definitions, but concepts capable of expansion and growth. The child's soul needs to be equipped with the kind of seeds that can continue to grow during the whole of the life to come. For this growth to take place, it is not enough just to apply certain principles in one's teaching; one has to know how to live with the child.

It is especially important for the moral and ethical aspect of education that we remember, for the ages between seven and fourteen, that the child's moral judgment should be approached only through an appeal to feelings called forth by verbal pictures illustrating the essentials of an inherent morality. What matters at this age is that the child should develop sympathy for the moral and antipathy for the immoral. To give children moral admonitions would be going against their nature, for they do not penetrate the souls of children. The entire future moral development is determined by those things that, through forming sympathies, become transformed into moral judgments. One single fact will show the importance of the teacher's right relationship to the child with regard to moral development. If one can educate with a discriminating, yet practical, sense of psychology, one will notice that, at a certain time around the ninth or tenth year (the exact age may vary in individual cases), the children's relationship to the world—an outcome of sympathies and antipathies that can be cultivated—will be such that they forget themselves. Despite a certain "physical egotism" (to give it a name), the child will still be fully open to environmental influences. Just as teachers need clear insight into the child's developmental stages when they use observational methods in object lessons with children of nine or ten, such insight is particularly important when it comes to moral education. If one pays sufficient attention to the more individual traits emerging in pupils, an interesting phenomenon can be observed at that age: the awareness that the child has a special need for help from the teacher. Sometimes a few words spoken by the child can be like a call for help. They can be the appropriate signal for a perceptive teacher, who now must find the right words to help the child over the hump. For the child is passing through a critical stage, when everything may depend on a few words spoken by the teacher to reestablish the right relationship between pupil and teacher.

What is happening at this time? By wrestling with language, the young person becomes aware, very consciously, for the first time that "There is a difference between myself and the world." (This is unlike the time during the first seven-year period when, unconsciously, the child first learned to refer to the self as "I.") The child now strongly demands a new orientation for body, soul, and spirit vis-à-vis the world. This awareness happens between the ninth and the tenth year. Again, unconsciously, the child has a remarkable experience in the form of all kinds of seemingly unrelated sentiments, feelings, and will impulses, which have no outward relationship with the behavior. The experience is: "Here before me stands my teacher who, as authority, opens the world for me. I look into the world through the medium of this authority. But is this authority the right one for me? Am I receiving the right picture of the world?" Please note that I am not saying this thought is a conscious one. All this happens subtly in the realm of the child's feelings. Yet this time is decisive for determining whether or not the child can feel the continued trust in the teacher's authority necessary for a healthy development until the onset of puberty. And this experience causes a certain inner unrest and nervousness in the child. The teacher has to find the right words to safeguard the child's continued confidence and trust. For together with this consolidation of trust, the moral character of the child also becomes consolidated. At first it was only latent in the child; now it becomes inwardly more anchored and the child attains inner firmness. Children grasp, right into the physical organism, something that they had perceived thus far as a self-evident part of their own individual self, as I described earlier.

Contemporary physiology, consisting on the one side of anthropology and on the other of an abstract psychology, is ignorant of the most fundamental facts. One can say that, until the second dentition, all organic formations and functions proceed from the nerve-and-sense system. Between the change of teeth and puberty, the child's physical fitness or weakness depends on the good functioning of the rhythmic system, on the breathing and blood circulation. Between the ninth and the tenth birthdays, what previously was still anchored primarily in the breathing, in the upper part of the organism, basically shifts over to the blood circulation; this is the time when the wonderful number relationship of one to four is being developed, in the approximately eighteen breaths and the seventy-two pulse beats per minute. This relationship between breathing and blood circulation becomes established at this time of life. However, it is only the outer expression of deep processes going on in the child's soul, and the reinforcement of the trust between teacher and child must become part of these processes, for through this trust the consolidation of the child's inner being also occurs.

These interactions between physiological and moral development must be described in detail if one wishes to speak of moral education and of the relationship between pedagogy and morality. As an educator, whether or not I am aware of this particular point in a child's life will determine whether or not I exercise a beneficial or a harmful influence for the rest of a person's life.

I should like to show, as a comparison, how things done at this stage continue to affect all of the rest of life. You may have noticed that there are people who, when they grow old, exert an unusual influence on those around them. That there are such people is generally known. Such people don't even need to say much when they are with others. Their mere presence is enough to bring what one may call an "air of blessing" to those around them. A grace emanates from them that brings about a relaxed and balanced atmosphere. If one has the patience and energy to trace the origin of this gift, one will find that it has developed out of a seed that came into being during childhood through a deeply felt respect for the authority of someone in charge. One could also describe it by saying that, in such a case, the child's moral judgment had been enhanced by a feeling of veneration that gradually reached the level of religious experience. If a child, between the change of teeth and puberty, experiences the feeling of reverence for certain people, reverence tinged even with a genuine religious feeling that lifts moral feelings into the light of piety, expressed in sincere prayer, then out of this childlike prayer grows the gift of blessing in old age, the gift of radiating grace to one's fellow human beings. Using pictorial language, one could say: Hands that have learned to pray in childhood have the gift of bestowing blessing in old age. These words, though symbolic and pictorial, nevertheless correspond to the fact that seeds planted in childhood can have an effect right to the end of life.

Now, for an example how the stages of human life are interrelated; one example in the moral realm is, as I said earlier, that the child's ability to form mental images in the thinking process develops along a continuous line. Only memory will take on a different character after the change of teeth. Language, on the other hand, becomes somehow inverted. Between the second dentition and puberty, the young person develops an entirely different relationship to language. This new relationship can be properly served by bringing to the child at this time the grammar and logic inherent in language. One can tackle practically every aspect of language if, instead of rashly bringing to consciousness the unconscious element of language from early childhood, one makes this translation in a way that considers the child.

But what about the third relationship: the young child's creation of an individual equilibrium with the external world after having learned to walk? Most people interpret the child's attempt to use the legs for the first time in a purely external and mechanistic way. It is not generally known, for example, that our ability for spatial imagination and our capacity for mathematical imagery is an upward projection of our limbs' potential movements into the intellectual sphere; in this projection, the head experiences, as mental activity, what is experienced in our limbs as movement. A deeply hidden soul element of the human being lives especially in this system of movement, a deep soul element linked to outer material forces.

After crawling on hands and knees, the child assumes the vertical position, lifting vertically the bodily axis, which in the case of the animals remains parallel to the Earth's surface. This upright achievement of the child is the physical expression of the moral potential for human will forces, which lift the human being above the level of the animals.

One day a comprehensive physiology, which is at the same time anthroposophy, will learn to understand that moral forces express themselves in the way a child performs physical movements in space. What the child achieves by assuming the upright posture and thus becoming free of the forces that keep the animal's spine parallel to the Earth's surface, what the child achieves by rising into a state of equilibrium in space, is the physical expression of the moral nature of its will energy. It is this achievement that makes the human individual into a moral being.

The objection may be raised that during sleep the position of the human spine is also parallel to the Earth's surface. However I am speaking here about the general human organization, and about the way spatial dimensions are organized into the human being. Through an accurate assessment of these matters, within this upright position the physical expression of human morality can be seen, which allows the human countenance to gaze freely into the world.

Let me compare what actually happens in the child with a certain phenomenon in nature. In the southern region of old

Austria, (now part of Italy) there is a river named the Poik, whose source is in the mountains. Suddenly this river disappears, completely vanishes from sight, and surfaces again later. What appears as the second river does not have its own source, but after its reemergence, people call it the Unz. The Unz disappears again, and resurfaces as a river called The Laibach. In other words, this river flows, unseen, in the depths of the Earth for part of its journey. Similarly, what the child has absorbed from its surroundings in its early years rests unperceived during childhood sleep. During the first years of life, when the child is unconsciously given over to moral forces inherent in the environment, the child acquires the ability to use the limbs in an upright position, thus becoming free of animality. What the child puts into this newly won skill is not noticeable between the change of teeth and puberty, but reappears as freedom in the making of moral judgements, as the freedom of human morality in the will sphere. If the teacher has cultivated the right moral sympathies and antipathies in the child at primary school age—without, however, being too heavy-handed—then, during the time before puberty, the most important aspects of the will can continue their "underground existence." The child's individual will, built on inner freedom, will eventually become completely a part of a human sense of responsibility, and will reappear after puberty so that the young person can be received as a free fellow human being. If the educator has refrained from handing down interdicts, and has instead planted sympathies and antipathies in the pupils' emotional baggage, but without infringing upon the moral will now appearing, the young person can transform the gifts of sympathies and antipathies according to individual needs. After puberty, the young person can transform what was given by others into moral impulses, which now come freely from individuality.

This is how to develop, out of real empathy with the human being, what needs to be done at each age and stage. If one does so properly between the seventh and fourteenth years by allowing moral judgements to mature in the pupil's life of feeling, what was given to the child properly with the support of authority will be submerged into the human sphere of free will. The human being can become free only after having been properly guided in the cultivation of moral sympathies and antipathies. If one proceeds in this manner regarding moral education, one stands beside the pupils so that one is only the motivator for their own self-education. One gives them what they are unconsciously asking for, and then only enough for them to become responsible for their own selves at the appropriate age, without any risk or danger to themselves.

The difficulty regarding moral education to which I drew your attention at the beginning of today's meeting, is solved in this way. One must work side by side with one's pupils, unselfishly and objectively. In other words, the aim should be never to leave behind a relic of one's own brand of morality in the psychological makeup of the pupils; one should try instead to allow them to develop their own sympathies and antipathies for what they consider morally right or wrong. This approach will enable them to grow rightly into moral impulses and will give them a sense of freedom at the appropriate age.

The point is to stand beside the child on the basis of an intimate knowledge and art of psychology, which is both an art of life and an art of spiritual endeavor. This will do justice not only to artistic, but also to moral education. But one should have due respect for the human being and be able to rightly evaluate a child's human potential. Then one's education will become a moral education, which means that the highest claim, the highest demand, for the question of morality and education is contained in the following answer: The right relationship between education and morality is found in a moral pedagogy whereby the entire art of education is itself a moral deed. The morality inherent in an art of education is the basis for a moral pedagogy.

What I have said so far applies to education in general, but it is nearest to our heart at the present time, when an understandable and justified youth movement has been growing apace. I will not attempt to characterize this youth movement properly in just a few words. For many of you here, I have done so already in various other places. But I wish to express my conviction that, if the older generation of teachers and educators knows how to meet the moral impulses of the younger generation on the basis of an art of education as outlined here, this problem of modern youth will find its proper solution. For in the final resort, the young do not wish to stand alone; they really want to cooperate with the older generation. But this cooperation needs to happen so that what they receive from their elders is different, something *other*, from what they can themselves bring; they need to be able to perceive it as the thing which their soul needs and which the older people can give.

Contemporary social life has created conditions regarding this question of the younger generation that I would characterize in this way: It is often said that the old should retain their previous youthful forces in order to get on better with the young. Today (present company, as always, excluded) the older generation appears excessively youthful, because its members have forgotten how to grow old properly. Their souls and spirits no longer know how to grow into their changed bodies. They carry into their aging bodies what they used to do in their young days, but the human garment of life no longer fits. If now the old and the young meet, the ensuing lack of understanding is not caused by old age as such, but, on the contrary, because the old have not grown old properly and, consequently, cannot be of much help to the young. The young expect that the old should have grown old properly, without appearing childish. When today's young meet their elders, they find them not very different from themselves. They are left with the impression that, although the old people have learned more in life, they do not seem to understand life more deeply, to be wiser. The young feel that the old have not used their age to become mature, that they have remained at the same human level as the young themselves. Youth expects that the old should have grown old in the right way.

For this concept to enter social life properly, a practical art of education is needed, which ensures that the seeds planted in education bear fruit right into ripe old age, as I have described it in various examples. One has to be able to unfold the appropriate life forces for each stage of life. One must know how to grow old. When the old understand how to grow old properly, they are full of inner freshness, whereas if they have become gray and wrinkled while remaining childishly immature, they cannot give anything to the young that the latter don't have already. This sheds some light on the present situation. One must only look at these things objectively. Basically, those who find themselves in this situation are quite innocent of the problems involved. What matters is that we tackle this most important and topical human problem by looking closely at our contemporary education, and in particular at the moral factor in education. Coming to terms with it is of great import, not only from the educational point of view, but for the entire social life.

When all is said and done, the moral education of the human being is the crown of all education and teaching. In *Faust*, Goethe puts the following strange words into the mouth of the Creator-God:

> The good person, in darkest aberration,
> is of the right path conscious still.

It is worth noting that although Goethe let these words be spoken by the Lord God Himself, pedantic minds could not resist nitpicking over them. They said, "'The good person, in darkest aberration … is conscious…'"; this is a contradiction in terms, for the darkest aberration is purely instinctive and certainly not conscious. How could Goethe write such words in his *Faust*?" So much for erudite barbarians. Well, I believe that Goethe knew very well what he had written in this sentence. He wanted to express the idea that, for those who look at the moral life without prejudice, morality is connected with the darkest depths of the human being, and that in this realm one approaches the most difficult area of the human being. In today's meeting, we saw for ourselves the difficulty of approaching moral issues in practical education. In these areas the darkest realms of the human being are encountered. Goethe clearly recognized this, but he also recognized that what the moral person can achieve only through the brightest rays of the spirit light, has to be attained in the darkest depths of the soul. I would like to think that Goethe's words consecrate the moral aspect of education, for what do they really say? They express a deep truth of life, into which I wish to condense all that has been said about the meaning of moral education.

I therefore will sum up in the sense of Goethe's words what I outlined for you today by concluding as follows: If you wish to enter the land of knowledge, you must follow the Spirit-light of day. You must work your way out of the darkness into the light. If you wish to find your way to the land of art, you must work your way, if not to the dazzling light of the Sun itself, at least into the colored brightness that Spirit-light radiates into the world. For in this light and in this light alone is everything turned into art.

However, it would be sad if, before becoming a morally good person, I first had to work my way toward these two goals. To become a morally good person, the innermost kernel of the human being has to be taken hold of down to its deepest recesses, for that is where the right orientation is needed. And the following must be said too: True, in our search for knowledge, we must work our way toward the light, and the pursuit of art means striving toward the colorful light of day; but it is equally true that, in the moral life, the human being who has found the right orientation can be a good person without light, and also without brightness; it is possible to be a good person through all the darkness and obscurity of life. If, as "the good person," one is "conscious of the right path still," one will be able to find the right way through all existing darkness, into the light and into all the colorful brightness of the world.

5

Introduction to a Eurythmy Performance of the Waldorf School Pupils

STUTTGART — MARCH 27, 1923

As a complement to the art of eurythmy, to which we were pleased to introduce you earlier, I will be speaking today about its pedagogical aspect. This subject has become an established and organic part of Waldorf pedagogy. When it was my task, on previous occasions, to justify including eurythmy as a compulsory subject in our curriculum, it seemed appropriate to speak of it in terms of an "ensouled and spirit-permeated form of gymnastics." However, I wish to emphasize right from the start that this remark must in no way be taken as derogatory as far as conventional gymnastics is concerned. It arose from the lack of a gymnasium, which initially prevented us from giving gymnastics its rightful place in the curriculum, in addition to eurythmy. Now that we are fortunate enough to have a gymnasium, gymnastics also is an obligatory subject.

I do not share the view once expressed to me by a very famous contemporary physiologist, after he had heard the introduction I often make before a school eurythmy performance. I had said that eurythmy was to be presented as an ensouled and spirit-imbued form of gymnastics, to be practiced along with the more physically centered conventional gymnastics, which also had its proper place. Afterward, the famous physiologist came to me, saying: "You declared that gymnastics, the way it is practiced today, has a certain justification. But I tell you that it is sheer barbarism!" Perhaps his words are justified, if they imply that this whole subject of gymnastics ought to be reviewed, having fallen prey to the materialistic attitude of our times. This, however, would be a very different issue. The point is that gymnastics, as it is taught in our schools, deals with physical movements and efforts of the human organism, which place the human body into a position of equilibrium relative to the outside world. The aim of gymnastics is that the human body, with its system of blood circulation and its potential physical movements, find the proper relationship to an outside space, which has its own forms and internal dynamics. Gymnastics is primarily concerned with adapting internal human dynamics, the human system of movement and blood circulation, to the dynamics of outside space. Gymnastics will find its proper and justified place in the school curriculum if and when one can find, both in freestanding exercises and in those using an apparatus, the appropriate orientation into world dynamics, seen also as human dynamics, for the human being stands as microcosm within the macrocosm.

On the other hand, eurythmy as an educational subject for children is very different. Eurythmy belongs more to the inner realm of the human organization. It can be seen as furthering and enhancing what is done in gymnastics. In eurythmy, the person works more with the qualitative and inner dynamics that play between breathing and blood circulation. The person doing eurythmy is oriented toward the transformation, into externalized movements of the human organism, of what is happening between internal breathing and blood circulation. In this way, the eurythmist gains an intimate relationship of body and soul to the self, and experiences something of the inner harmony inherent in the human being. This experience, in turn, brings about greater inner stability and firmness because the essence of the ensouled and spirit-imbued movement works on the entire human being. Conventional gymnastics mainly activates the physical part of the human being and, in its own way, indirectly affects the soul and spirit of the athlete, whereas eurythmy activates the whole human being as body, soul, and, spirit. Eurythmy movements cause the human soul and spirit to flow into every physical movement. Just as speech and song embody laws inherent in one part of the human being, so eurythmy embodies laws inherent in the whole human being; similarly, eurythmy works on the young child as a matter of course just as the organic forces inherent in speech work and flow through the young child.

Children learn to speak because of the stimulation of sounds coming from outside, and the children's innate impulse to form sounds. Experience has shown that when children are introduced to eurythmy at the right age, they feel at home in its movements, with the same natural readiness as children finding their way into speech. An essential human feature—or, as I would like to call it, the *most* essential human feature—is developed and widened in this way. And since all education and training should aim at getting hold of the innate human being through the pupil's own self, we feel justified in using eurythmy as a form of ensouled and spirit-imbued gymnastics in its own right, even though it originated and was at first cultivated only as an art form within the anthroposophical movement.

The following may seem a little difficult to understand at first, but if we can recognize how, in accordance with human nature, the child incorporates into the organism what is derived from eurythmy lessons—complemented by musical and sculptural activities—one can see how all these elements affect the child's organism, and how they all work back again upon the entire nature of the child. One sees the child's faculty of cognition becoming more mobile and receptive through the influence of eurythmic exercises. Children develop a more active ideational life, opening with greater love toward what comes to meet them; and so, by using eurythmy in appropriate ways, the teacher has the possibility of training the children's powers of mental imagery.

Eurythmy also works back very powerfully on the will, and especially on the most intimate traits of the human will. For instance, it is easy enough to lie with words, and there are many ways of counteracting such a weakness in children, merely by speaking to them. But in such a case one can also make profitable use of eurythmy, for if, as a eurythmist, one lets words flow directly into physical movements so that they become visible speech, it becomes very evident that the use of this medium simply cancels out the possibility of lying. The possibility of lying ceases when one begins to experience what is involved in revealing the soul through one's physical movements. Consequently one will come to see that, with regard to the human will, truthfulness, which is of such great ethical importance, can be developed particularly well with the aid of eurythmy exercises. To sum up, one can say that eurythmy is a kind of gymnastics developed out of the domain of the human soul and that it gives back to the soul, in turn, very much indeed. This is the reality of eurythmy and its specific character. Eventually it will be regarded quite naturally as an intrinsic part of education. We have no doubt that it will happen. However, these things take their time because the public first needs to overcome built-in prejudices. There will be those who say, "Look at this handful of crazies," but such has always been the way of the world. There once were a handful of people among whom one crazy fellow actually maintained that the Sun stood in the center of the universe and that the planets, together with the Earth, were revolving around it. Such a crazy idea was at first totally rejected, for no one of a sane mind would contemplate such nonsense. Nevertheless, during approximately the first third of the nineteenth century there was quite a following for this "crazy" idea, which Copernicus had asked to be taken as the truth. Why should one not wait patiently until something that cannot even be proved as convincingly as the Copernican system of the universe is accepted by society at large!

Eurythmy feeds back into the child's cognitive faculties, endowing them with greater mobility, causing a keener interest and a sense of truthfulness; it feeds back into the human emotional disposition, which lives between the faculties of cognition and a person's will capacity. It is tremendously important that the human being, with the aid of eurythmy, be able to keep hold of the self as a whole, instead of living in the dichotomy of soul and spirit on one side, and human physical existence on the other.

One could keep asking forever, "What is the relationship between body and soul?" It is downright comical to see the question coming up again and again! There have been no end of attempts to construct theoretical explanations of how the one side affects the other. But if this matter can be experienced directly—which happens when one does eurythmy—the question immediately assumes a different character. The question then becomes: How does an intrinsic unity composed of body, soul, and spirit come to work in separate ways, on the one side as soul element and on the other side as physical element? Getting hold of these interactions completely forces one to reshape the question altogether. Then, there is no need for theorizing, for everything is founded on practical experience and in accordance with reality. Some people have the opinion that anthroposophy deals with "cloud-cuckoo-land," whereas in fact, anthroposophy aims at working directly into practical life.

Nowadays, the spirit in matter is no longer perceived; as a result, the nature of matter is no longer understood. This nature can be comprehended only by *doing*. This may suggest how eurythmy affects the child. One can say that, when doing eurythmy, children, through the will, gets hold of the inner harmony between the upper more spiritual side of the human being and the lower more physical side, so that will initiative is being created. And will initiative is the very thing that needs to be cultivated in today's education. Those who observe the psychological development of our times know very well that there is a great lack of will initiative. It is badly needed in the social sphere, and the art that will bring it about os most needed in pedagogical practice.

The things I have indicated briefly, you will be able to witness for yourselves while watching the children of the Waldorf school perform eurythmy. I hope that what you see on the stage, done with youthful joy and vigor, confirms what I have tried to put into words for you.

6

Why Base Education on Anthroposophy?

DORNACH — JUNE 30, 1923

PART ONE

It gives me great pleasure to talk to teachers once again about education, so may I welcome you all most warmly, especially those in this audience who are actively engaged in teaching.

The pedagogy that arises from anthroposophy is neither theoretical nor utopian, but one of practice and application; so you will appreciate that two brief lectures allow me to give only a few outlines. Some time ago, during a longer conference of Swiss teachers here at the Goetheanum, I took the liberty of speaking about education at greater length; but even then the allotted time proved too short. During that conference there was greater opportunity to go into details than is possible in only two sessions, and much of teaching is precisely about details. Nevertheless, I shall try to describe at least a few aspects, especially about our chosen theme: Why base education on anthroposophy?

This question is bound to come up for the most varied reasons. To begin with, it will be asked because anthroposophy is still often regarded as a form of sectarianism and as a philosophy of life suited to the personal tastes of certain people. The question will then be: Should education be influenced at all by a particular worldview? Can any fruitful results be expected when people draw conclusions for education from their particular beliefs or ideas? If such a question were justified, then what we may call anthroposophical pedagogy would probably not exist at all.

Now it happens to be the case that in this century every religion and every philosophy of life has developed its own particular ideas or set up its own particular demands about education. And one can always discern the underlying ideological background in educational institutions.

This, however, is exactly what an anthroposophical education should make impossible. Let me begin by mentioning that for a number of years now in Stuttgart, we have tried to run a primary and secondary school in the spirit of anthroposophical ways of teaching. To a certain extent, our ideal there has been that everything should proceed naturally and in harmony with human nature and its development, and thus no one should even consider it the realization of some anthroposophical idea, or that any particular brand of philosophy is being disseminated there.

The reason this question comes up at all is that, when something is represented before the world, one is obligated to name it. But I assure you that I would personally prefer that what is being represented here at the Goetheanum needed no name at all, or if one were free to call it one name now, and later another. For we are concerned here, not with certain ideas that usually underlie a view of the world, but with a certain mode of research and a way of viewing life that could be given many different names from the most varied standpoints. Actually, the names they are usually given tend to be misleading anyway.

I will illustrate this with a rather trivial example, which may nevertheless help you to understand what I mean. When it comes to naming spiritual movements and so on, humanity is no further along than it was with personal names a few centuries ago in Europe, when a person's last name was a literal reference to physical characteristics or line of work. By now we have forgotten the origins of these names, just as they should have been forgotten. (Keep in mind that the following example is quite trivial!) There once was a famous linguist whose name was Max Müller [Miller]. Now suppose someone had mentioned a "Miller," a person (referring to the linguist) living in such and such a house; and suppose another person overhearing this proceeded to take sacks of grain to that address hoping to have it milled!

Most of us know better than to take people's names literally. But when it comes to spiritual movements, that's just what we do. Instead of looking for fundamentals, we analyze the names and base our ideas on them. So one analyzes and interprets the name anthroposophy and then forms a view of it. Just as the word "miller" has little relevance in the case of the great linguist of that name, so does the word "anthroposophy" cover only a small portion of what is intended to be a spiritual science and a spiritual view of life. Hence, as I've said, I would prefer to give a new name every day to the spiritual research accomplished and to the spiritual lifestyle practiced here. For the very multitude of names would be an outer expression of their essential reality. At best, what we can do is to characterize more or less fully what anthroposophy wishes to contribute to today's world. It is not possible to give a definition of it that, by itself, would make sense. Today and tomorrow I will try to show, at least to some extent, how anthroposophy can become fruitful for the education and training of the growing child. The description I shall give will necessarily be rather incomplete, for the fullness of what is intended cannot possibly be communicated in only two lectures.

If we look around today with real interest in the spiritual development of the world, we find ourselves in a whirl of demands, programs, and ideas, all clamoring for attention. Among them is the question of education. Schemes for reform emerge one after another, their authors all more or less well qualified for this task, and more often than not they are mere dabblers. Whatever the case, this phenomenon demonstrates a deep and real need for clear insights about questions of education.

However, this phenomenon is connected with another fact; it is exceedingly difficult today to come to satisfactory, let alone fruitful, ideas about the treatment of the growing human being. And if we want to see why there is so much talk of educational reform and educational ideas today, we need to look a little more deeply into some aspects of our modern civilization.

If we look, on the one hand, at material life today and, on the other, at spiritual life, the life of mind and thought, we find that tremendous advances have been made in practical life through technology, yet there is a deep gulf, a deep abyss, between the realm of scientific theory—that is, what one has to learn if one wishes to be an educated person—and that of practical life situations. More and more in modern life a peculiar trend has developed regarding the subjects studied and practiced in our academic and educational institutions.

Take the sphere of medicine, for example. Young medical students go through their course of studies. They learn what modern science has to offer. Along with their studies, they also undergo much "practical" laboratory and hospital training. And yet, when medical students have passed their final examinations, they still have to go through a period of clinical practice. That is to say, the final examination is not sufficient for the student to be recognized as a qualified doctor in practical medicine. Moreover, doctors in general find that remarkably little of all the theoretical work they went through to begin with finds useful applications in actual practice.

I have chosen medicine as an example, but I could equally well have shown the same trend in almost every academic profession. Nowadays, when we have acquired a certain training in one sphere or another, we still have a large gap to bridge before we become proficient in the various practical fields. This is so in almost every sphere. It applies not only to the medical student, but also to the technical student, the barrister, or the student of commerce and economics; and, above all, it applies to the teacher. In the learned and scientific climate of our age, teachers have been introduced to the theory of education in more or less scientific and psychological terms. Having attained a certain standard in educational theory and knowledge, teachers still have to find their own way into practical teaching.

What I have said so far can, most likely, be accepted as a correct assessment of the situation. There is, however, something else that will not be accepted quite so readily: the gulf is so great between theoretical learning, which occupies the main part of our intellectual life today, and the practical aspects of life, that this gulf cannot be bridged in any field except one. The single exception is the technical and engineering profession, whose members have to fulfill the most stringent tests. If the structure of a bridge is sound in theory, but faulty in other ways, it will collapse when the first train crosses it. In this case, natural laws inexorably react to anything that is wrong. In this field a person is forced to acquire practical expertise.

But when we deal with the human being, we find ourselves in a different situation. Here it is definitely impossible to answer the question of how many patients a doctor has treated correctly and how many have been treated wrongly, for in this case there is little possibility of conclusive proof. If we now consider education, we may well hold the opinion that there already is excessive criticism and that teachers have plenty to put up with! But it will hardly be possible to ascertain whether, according to the facts of life, a given educational method has been right or wrong. For life's answers are not as cut and dried as those we receive from dead, mineral nature. Nevertheless, there is generally a justified feeling that the way to the acquisition of the theory of education is not necessarily a direct road to practical experience. If there is one domain in the world that demonstrates the blind alley that such a gap between theory and practice forces us into, it is everything that pertains to the human being.

During the last few centuries, and especially in the nineteenth century, we have developed a scientific spirit. Every human being, even the supposedly illiterate, exists amid this scientific spirit. All our thinking is in this mode. Yet see how alienated from the world this spirit is; what a pity the last few years have been, as world history rolled over us in powerful waves, facing us with immensely significant facts; how pitiable it was to see that people, no matter how clever their theories, cannot make anything of the path life has actually taken! At the beginning of the war, did we not hear brilliant economists declare: "Economic science teaches us that the commercial and other economic relations of the world are now so closely interwoven that a war could last at most a few months?" The facts contradicted these false predictions—the war actually continued several years. The thoughts people had arrived at out of their scientific reasoning, the speculations they had made about the course of world events, none of those were in the least applicable to the events themselves.

The human being, growing into life and appearing before us in what I should like to call the most sublime form as child, cannot be understood by a culture that has produced such a gulf between theory and practice.

Only very rigid materialists would imagine that what grows up in the child can be reduced to physical bodily development.

We look with immense devotion and reverence at the manifestations of the creative powers that appear before us in the child during the first few weeks of life. Everything in the child is still indefinite in character then, and yet what the child will achieve in later life already lives innately in the baby. We look at growing children as, over weeks, months, and years, they unfold forces out of inner being. We see these forces make the individual features of the child more and more distinct, movements more and more coordinated and purposeful. In this developing human being, we see the whole riddle of creation revealing itself most wonderfully before our eyes. We see the first unfocused look in a little child's eyes and watch them grow full of inner warmth, of inner fire, as the child becomes active; we see the at first imprecise motions of arms and fingers, we see them turning most beautifully meaningful, like letters in an alphabet. And seeing all this with real human interest forces us to acknowledge that there is more at work here than physical nature; soul and spirit are at work behind it. Every particle of the human being is at the same time a manifestation of soul and spirit. Every shade of color in the child's cheek expresses something of soul and spirit. It is completely impossible to understand this coloring of the cheek merely on a material basis, impossible to understand it at all, if we do not know how the soul pours itself into the pink color of the cheek. Here, spirit and physical nature are one.

We simply bypass children if we now approach them with today's old encrusted outlook on life, with its open gulf between theoretical pursuits and practical application. Neither theories nor instincts can make sense of the child; in any case, in our civilization the instincts cannot comprehend the spirit. Modern life has separated our spiritual pursuits from the physical world, and in so doing, our spiritual aims have become abstract theory.

And so abstract theories about education have arisen, Herbartian pedagogy, for instance—in its way full of spirit, and theoretically grand, but unable to actively penetrate real life.[1] Or else, in all our attempts to live in the spiritual realm, we go astray, deciding we will have nothing to do with any scientific pedagogy at all, and rely instead on our educational instincts— something many people today propose.

There is another phenomenon of our age that shows how much this gulf between our theoretical understanding of the spiritual and our comprehension of practical needs has estranged us from true human nature. Modern science has evolved most remarkably, and, naturally enough, saw a need to create a scientific pedagogy. But it had no way of reaching the growing human being, the child. Science has much to say about the sensory world, but the more it did so in the modern age, the less it could say anything about the human being. Thus, on the model of the natural sciences, human beings were experimented on. Experimental pedagogy came into being.

What is the significance of this urge for experimental pedagogy? Please do not misunderstand me. I have no objections to experimental psychology or to experimental pedagogy as such. Scientifically, they can accomplish a great deal. In theory they provide excellent results. The point here is not to judge these things critically, but to see what tendency of our time they express. We will have to continue experimenting with the child in an external fashion to find out how memory, will forces, and powers of attention work in one child or another; external experiments are necessary because we have lost touch

---

1. Johann Friedrich Herbart (1776–1841), German philosopher and educator. He developed a a general metaphysical theory of pluralistic realism with important psychological implications, which rejected concepts of faculties and innate ideas; his theory became the basis for a pedagogy, about which he wrote several books.

with the inner human being. People can no longer meet and mingle with their fellow human beings, soul to soul, and so they try to do this through experiment, to read from bodily reactions the expressions of the soul that they can no longer approach directly. Today's experimental pedagogy and psychology are living proof that our science is powerless when it tries to approach the whole human being, who is spirit, soul, and body, all in one.

We must take these things seriously if we wish to deal with modern questions of schooling and education, for they will slowly help us realize that genuine progress in this field depends first and foremost on a true knowledge of the human being. But such a knowledge will not be attained unless we bridge the gulf between theory and practice, which has widened to such an appalling extent. The theories we have today deal only with the human physical body, and whenever we try to approach the human soul and spirit, we fail despite all our frantic efforts. Soul and spirit must be investigated by ways other than the recognized scientific methods of today. To gain insight into human nature, we must follow a different path from the one commonly upheld as the standard of scientific exactitude and accuracy. The task of anthroposophy is to approach the true human nature, to search for a real knowledge of the human being, which sees spirit, soul, and body as a whole. Anthroposophy sets out to know again not only the physical aspect of the human being, but also the whole human being.

Unfortunately there is as yet little realization of where the real tasks lie—the tasks that life in its fullness sets us. I will give you one example to point out where our attention must turn, if real knowledge of the human being is once more to be attained. When I was young—a very long time ago—among other views of the world, one emerged that was initiated by the physicist Ernst Mach.[2] This philosophy became very well known at the time. What I am about to say is intended only as an example, and I ask you to treat it as such. The essential point in Mach's argument follows. He said:

It is nonsense to speak of a thing-in-itself, such as, for example, an "atom." It is also nonsense to speak of an "I," existing as a "thing" within ourselves. We can speak only of sensations. Who has ever perceived an atom? One can perceive red, blue, and yellow, or perceive C-sharp, G, and A in music; one perceives sour, sweet, and bitter tastes. We perceive with the sense of touch hard or soft things. In a nutshell, we perceive only sensations. When we make a picture of the world, it is made up of nothing but sensations. And if we then look into ourselves, there, too, we find sensations and only sensations. There is nothing beyond sensations—sensations that we then link together. A soft velvety feeling associated with the redness of a rose, the sensation of being burned with the reddish appearance in a red-hot poker—in every case, sensations are linked one to another.

So much for Ernst Mach. One must admit that, compared to the idea of an atomic world, which of course no one can see, Mach's idea was, in his time, a true advance. Today this idea has been forgotten again. But I am not going to speak of the

---

2. Ernst Mach (1838–1916), Austrian physicist and philosopher, professor in Prague and Vienna. He researched, in physics, questions of physiology and psychology of the senses, especially in relation to a theory of knowledge. He developed *Empiriokritizismus*, a philosophy of "realism," based on the analysis of sensation. He also studied projectiles, and his name is used to refer to the speed of sound.

idea itself. I am going to take this case only as an example of the nature of the human being.

Ernst Mach once told the story of how he came to his view of things. He reached the core of his views when he was a youth of seventeen. He was out for a walk on an exceptionally hot summer day, when it dawned upon him that the whole notion of "things-in-themselves" is really superfluous in any view of the world; it is "the fifth wheel of the cart," as the saying goes. Out in the world, there are only sensations. They merge with the sensations of our own bodily nature, our own human being. In the outer world the sensations are connected rather more loosely, in the inner life more firmly, thus conjuring the idea of "I." Sensations, and nothing but sensations. This is what flashed through the boy of seventeen on a hot summer day. According to him, all he did later was to elaborate and expand the theory. But his whole worldview came to him in a flash, as described, on a hot day in summer, when he suddenly felt himself merging with the scent of the rose, the redness of the rose, and so on.

Now, if it had been just a little hotter, this whole philosophy of one's own being flowing together with sensations might never have arisen at all, for good old Mach as a youth of seventeen might have been overcome by light-headedness, or, if hotter still, he might have suffered sunstroke! We thus have three successive stages a person might go through: The first stage is evolving a certain philosophy, conceived in a somewhat flushed and loosened inner condition; the second, feeling faint; and the third, is the possibility of suffering a sunstroke.

If contemporary scholars were to take up the task of discovering externally how a man like the learned Mach had arrived at his view of the world, I can easily imagine they would think of all sorts of things, such as what Mach had studied, who his teachers were, what his dispositions and his talents were, and so on; but they would hardly have placed in the foreground of their argument the significant fact that he had passed through the first of the three stages mentioned. And yet, this fact actually happened, as he relates himself. What was its real basis?

You see, unless you can understand a phenomenon like this, you cannot expect to know the human being proper. What was it that happened when the seventeen-year-old Mach went for a walk? Evidently he grew very hot. He was midway between feeling comfortably warm and being hot enough to lose consciousness. Now, we have no proper knowledge of such a condition unless we know from anthroposophical research that the human being has not only a physical body, but, above and beyond it, a supersensible, invisible body, which I have described in my books as the etheric or formative-forces body. Today, of course, I cannot relate all the research on which the assumption of this supersensible formative-forces body rests, but you can read about it in the anthroposophical literature. It is as secure and well established a result of scientific research as any other.

Now what about this etheric body? In the waking state we are ordinarily entirely dependent on our physical body. Materialists are quite right in stating that the thought the human being evolves in the physical world is connected to the brain or nervous system. We do need the physical body for ordinary thinking. But the moment we deviate even a little from this ordinary thinking to a certain freedom of inner life and experience, as in the case, for example, of exercising artistic imagination, the almost imperceptible activity of the etheric body grows more intense. Therefore, if a person is thinking in the ordinary "matter-of-fact" way (we must do so in ordinary life, and I am really not speaking of it in a derogatory sense), then thinking must occur mainly with the organs of the physical body, while the etheric body is called into play only to a lesser extent.

But if I switch to imaginative creation, let us say to poetic creation, the physical body sinks a little into the background, while human ideation, using the etheric body, grows more mobile and active during this process. The various viewpoints are joined together in a more living way, and the whole inner being acquires a mobility greater than in the exercise of ordinary, matter-of-fact, everyday thinking.

The decision to think creatively, imaginatively, is subject to one's free choice. But there is something else that is not so much subject to free choice, that might be caused by external conditions. If a person becomes very warm, the activity of the physical body, including thinking, decreases, while that of the etheric body becomes more and more lively. Thus, when Mach at the age of seventeen went for a walk and was subjected to the oppressive heat of the sun, his etheric body simply grew more active. All other physicists developed their science of physics with the physical body predominant. The heat of the Sun so affected the young Mach that he could think, not unlike the other physicists, but with more flowing concepts: "The whole world consists of nothing but sensations!"

Had the heat been even more intense, the connection between his physical body and his etheric body would have been loosened to such an extent that the good Mach would no longer have been able to think with his etheric body either, or even to be active at all. The physical body ceases to think when it is too hot and, if the heat increases further, becomes ill and suffers a sunstroke.

I give you this example because it enables us to see how necessary it is to understand that a supersensible limb in the human being plays a vital part in the person's activities. This supersensible limb is the etheric, or formative forces, body, which gives us form (our shape and our figure), maintains the forces of growth in us, and so on.

Anthroposophy further shows that there are still other super-sensible members in the human being. Please do not be stopped by the terms we use. Beyond the formative forces of the etheric body, we have the astral body, which is the vehicle of sensation, and, in addition to these three "bodies," we come to the true I-being, the ego. We must learn to know not just the human being's physical body; we must also come to a practical knowledge of the interactions between the human being's other bodies.

Anthroposophy takes this step from what is accessible to the senses (which contemporary science worships exclusively) to what is accessible to the higher senses. This is not done from any mystical or fanciful inclination, but from the same disciplined scientific spirit that orthodox science also uses. Physical science applies this strictness of approach only to the world of the senses and to the concrete intellectual activity bound to the physical body. Anthroposophy, through an equally strict scientific process, evolves a knowledge, a perception, and therewith a feeling, for the supersensible.

This process does not lead merely to the existence of yet another science beyond accustomed science and learning. Anthroposophy does not provide us with another form of science of the spirit, which again might represent a theory. If one rises to the supersensible, science remains no longer a theory, but of its own accord assumes a practical nature. Science of the spirit becomes a knowledge that flows from the whole human being. Theory takes hold only of the head, but knowledge of the human being involves the human being as a whole. Anthroposophy gives us this knowledge, which is really more than just knowledge. What then does it teach us?

From anthroposophy, we learn to know what is contained in the etheric or formative-forces body, and we learn that we cannot stop short with the rigid definitions applied to the physical world today. All our concepts begin to grow mobile. Then a person who looks at the world of plants, for example, with this living, mobile knowledge, sees not merely fixed forms that could be rendered in a drawing, but living forms in the process of transformation. All of my conceptual life grows inwardly mobile. I feel the need for a lively freshness, because I no longer look at the plant externally; in thinking of it, I become one with its growth, its springing and its sprouting. In my thoughts I become spring in the spring, autumn in the autumn. I do not just see the plant springing from the soil and adorning itself with flowers, or the leaves fading, growing brown, and falling to the ground; not only do I see, but I also participate in the entire process. As I look out at the budding, sprouting plant in the springtime, and as I think and form ideas of it, my soul is carried along and joins in the sprouting and budding processes. My soul has an inner experience as if all concepts were becoming sun-like. Even as I penetrate deeper and deeper into the plant nature, my thoughts strive continually upward to the sunlight. I become inwardly alive.

In such an experience we become human beings whose souls are inwardly alive, instead of dry theoreticians. When the leaves lose their colors and fall to the ground, we go through a similar experience, through a kind of mourning. We ourselves become spring, summer, autumn, and winter. In our innermost soul, we feel cold with the snow as it falls on the earth, covering it with its veil of white. Instead of remaining in the realm of arid, dead thoughts, everything is enlivened within us.

When we speak of what we call the *astral body*, some people become scornful of the idea, thinking it a crackpot theory, a figment of someone's imagination. But this is not the case. It is something observed as is anything in the real world. If this is really understood, one begins to understand something else too. One begins, for example, to understand love as inner experience, the way love weaves and works through all existence. As the physical body mediates an inner experience of cold or warmth, so the experience of the astral body grants an inner perception of whether love or antipathy is weaving and working. These experiences enrich our whole lives.

However much you study the many fashionable theories today, you cannot say that what you have studied is absorbed by your full human being. It usually remains a possession of the head. If you want to apply it, you must do so according to some external principle. On the other hand, anthroposophical study passes into your whole being like the blood running throughout your whole body; it is the substance of life that penetrates you, the spiritual substance of life, if I may use such a contradictory expression. You become a different human being when you take on anthroposophy.

Take a part of the human body, let's say this finger. The most it can do is touch. In order to do what the eye does, it would have to organize itself very differently. The eye, like the finger, consists also of tissues, but the eye has become inwardly selfless, inwardly transparent, and thus it mediates the outside world for human perception.

When someone has internalized the essence of the astral body, the astral body also becomes a means for perceiving what is out there; it becomes an "eye of the soul." Such a person then looks into the soul of another, not in any superstitious or magical way, but in a perfectly natural way. Thus, a perception of what is in the soul of another human being takes place consciously, a perception that in ordinary situations is achieved, unconsciously, only in love. Contemporary science separates theory from practice. Anthroposophy introduces knowledge directly into the stream of life.

When studying anthroposophy, it is inconceivable to study first and then have to go through a practical course. It would be a contradiction in terms, for anthroposophy in its wholeness penetrates the soul and spirit just as blood penetrates the growing and developing human embryo. It is a reality.

This knowledge will not lead us to engage in external experiments on other human beings, but will introduce us to the inner texture of the soul. It gives us a real approach to our fellow human beings. And then we also learn something else; we learn to recognize the degree of intimacy in the relationship between human conceptual life and human physical growth.

What does contemporary psychology know about this relationship? On the one hand, one talks of how concepts or ideas are formed; on the other hand, physiologists talk about how the human being grows. But they know nothing at all of the close and intimate connection between the two, between physical growth and conceptual activity. Hence, they do not know what it means to bring the wrong kinds of concepts to a child between the ages of seven and fourteen. They do not know how harmfully this affects the bodily growth processes. They do not realize how growth processes are hindered if the child is forced to memorize too many facts. Nor do they know that in giving the child too little to remember, they encourage an overactivity of the growth processes, which can also cause certain illnesses. This intimate connection between the body and the supersensible soul force is simply not known. Without such knowledge, education and teaching remain a mere groping about in the dark. Originally the aim of anthroposophy was by no means to produce a new form of education. The aim was to provide a real understanding of the human being and, in so doing, the educational side arose almost out of its own accord.

In looking around at the reformist ideas that have arisen here and there in our time, we find that they are all well meant, and many of them deserve the greatest respect. Reformers cannot help, to begin with, that they do not possess a real and true knowledge of the human being. Were there such a knowledge behind the various schemes for educational reform, there would be no need for anthroposophy to say anything. On the other hand, if there were a real knowledge of the human being, this in itself would be nothing but anthroposophy with a different name.

In the absence of true knowledge of the human being in our modern civilization as a whole, anthroposophy came to fill the gap. Education can be based only on a knowledge of the human being. It can be fruitful only if one doesn't separate theory from practice, and if, instead, knowledge passes into activity, as in the case of a true artist, into creative activity. It can bear fruit only if all knowledge is art—if, instead of being a science, educational science becomes an art, the art of education. Such an active form of knowledge of the human being must then become the basis of all educational work.

This is why there is an anthroposophical pedagogy at all. Not because certain people are fanatics of anthroposophy, thinking of it as some "jack of all trades" that can do everything, and therefore, among other things, can also educate children! Anthroposophical pedagogy exists because it is inherently necessary. An art of education can grow only from a realistic, mature knowledge of the human being, the knowledge that anthroposophy attempts to provide. This is why we have an anthroposophical art of education.

Following this introduction, we will return tomorrow to this subject.

7

Why Base Education on Anthroposophy?

DORNACH — JULY 1, 1923

PART TWO

Last night I tried to show how the deep gulf between practical life and spiritual-cultural life (the latter being very theoretical at this point) hinders modern teachers from discovering a true art of teaching. The effects of this contemporary phenomenon are not generally taken seriously enough because the intellect is unaware of the true situation, a situation revealed to the human mind and soul only over the course of life. There is a strong tendency these days to remain deaf to all that the human sensibility would tell us. We are more easily prepared to listen to the voice of the intellect.

People today feel compelled to grant unlimited and infallible authority to science, which is actually only a science of physical nature and not a science of the soul and spirit. This is true, because in every connection the intellect has been set up to judge everything, including things that do not proceed from the intellect alone, but from the whole human being. Teachers, no less than other people, are the products of our whole civilization's approach to cultural-spiritual life, and the feelings and sensibility they bring to their work in the schools come directly from what they themselves had to endure in school. Yet, when they are with their children in a classroom situation, they are very keenly and intensely aware of the influence of the gulf I already mentioned.

Teachers have learned all kinds of things about the human soul and how it works. Their own feeling and will impulses have been shaped accordingly, as well as the whole tone and frame of mind brought to their work as teachers. And beyond all of this, they are expected to base their work on extremely theoretical notions of mind and soul.

It is not very useful to say: Theory? Certainly a teacher's work in school comes from the whole human heart! Of course it does, in an abstract sense. It is very easy to make such a statement abstractly. You might as well suggest that a person jump into the water without getting wet. We have the same chance of jumping into the water and not getting wet as we have of finding help in meeting the fresh souls of children within today's academic institutional teachings about the human soul and spirit. Just as certain as you will get wet if you jump into water, so will the teacher, having assimilated the academic learning of today, be a stranger to everything that belongs to soul and spirit. This is a simple fact. And the primary concern of all who would practice the art of teaching should be the recognition of this fact in its full human significance.

Teachers who have gone through a modern academic education may be prepared to meet the child with sincere human feelings, with sympathies and an earnest desire to work with and for humanity; but when they have a little child before them—the "becoming" human being—they feel as if everything they have assimilated theoretically has failed to warm their hearts and strengthen their will for spiritual activity. At best, all of that theory will enable them merely to "hover around the child," as it were, instead of providing an opening for them to meet the child.

Thus, teachers enter their classrooms as if surrounded by a wall they cannot cross to reach the children's souls; they busy themselves with the air around the children, and cannot accompany, with their own souls, the in-breathing process through which the air enters the child. They feel like outsiders to the children, splashing about, as it were, in an ill-defined theoretical element outside the child. Or again, when teachers stand in front of children, they feel that everything they learned intellectually from our excellent natural science (which gives us such strong and clear understanding of the mineral world) does not help them at all to find their way to the child. It tells them something about the bodily nature of the child, but even this is not fully understood unless they reach down to the underlying spiritual element, because the spiritual element is the foundation of all corporeality.

Thus it happens that those who wish to approach the child in a pedagogical way are led to engage in external physical experiments. They use trial-and-error methods, testing for things related to the child's body so that the memory forces are developed properly; they try to find out how to treat the child's physical body in order to exercise the child's powers of concentration and so on. The teacher begins to feel like one who, instead of being led into the light, is given dark glasses that almost cut out the light completely, for science manages to make even the physical nature of the human being opaque. It does not and cannot enable a teacher to reach the real being of children with their natural spirit-filled soul life.

These things are not yet discussed rationally in our present civilization. Where else will you hear what I have been saying—that without a proper and true knowledge of the human being, and despite our remarkable knowledge of physical phenomena, we simply bypass the child, who remains alien? And because no one else can say this, anything that could be said on the matter finds expression in feelings and sentiments instead of in human speech. Consequently, teachers go away from almost every lesson with a certain feeling of inner dissatisfaction. This feeling may not be very pronounced, but it accumulates and tends to harden them, causing them to be, not just strangers to the child, but strangers to the world, with their hearts and minds growing cold and prosaic.

And so we see freshness, life, and mobility vanishing because of a lack of intimate human contact between the adult teacher and the growing child. These things need to be considered and understood intellectually, but also with the teacher's full humanity. Today's intellectual understanding, schooled only in outer, sense phenomena, has become too coarse to get a hold on these more intimate soul connections in all their refinement and tenderness.

When the art of teaching is discussed, we hear the old demands echoing again and again; as you well know, pedagogy is derived on the one hand from psychology, from the science of the soul, and on the other from ethics, the science of human, moral responsibility. Educational theorists, when speaking of the art of teaching, tell us that education should be based on two main pillars: the science of the soul and the science of ethics. But all we really have is something that falls between the two. It is a complete illusion to believe that a true science of the soul exists today. We need to remind ourselves repeatedly of the phrase, "a soulless science of the soul," coined in the nineteenth century, because human beings no longer have the power to penetrate the soul. For what is our present science of the soul? I may sound paradoxical if I say what it really is.

In the past, human beings had a science of the soul that sprang from original instincts, from clairvoyant knowledge then common to all humanity. This clairvoyant knowledge of ancient times was primitive, pictorial, mythical; nonetheless, it deeply penetrated the human soul. Ancient people possessed such a science of the soul; they had a feeling, an intuitive sense for what a soul is. And they coined words that bear a true relation to the human soul, for example, the words *thinking*, *feeling*, and *willing*. Today, however, we no longer have the inner life that can truly animate these words.

What does anthroposophy show us about thinking? As human beings, thinking equips us with thoughts. But the thoughts we have today in our ordinary civilized life appear as if, instead of looking at the face of someone we meet, we look at that person only from behind. When we speak of thoughts today, we see only the "rear view," as it were, of what really lives in thought. Why is this so?

When you look at a person from behind, you see, of course, a certain shape and form, but you do not learn about the person's physiognomy. You do not see the side where the soul life is outwardly expressed. If you learn to know thoughts the usual way in this scientific age, you come to know the rear view only, not the inner human being. If, however, you look at thoughts from the other side, they retain their life and remain active forces.

What are these thoughts? They are the same as the forces of growth in the human being. Seen externally, thoughts are abstract; seen internally, we find the same forces in them by which the little child grows bigger, whereby a child receives form and shape in the limbs, in the body, in the physiognomy. These are the thought forces. When we look externally, we see only dead thoughts; in a similar way, when we view a person's back, we do not see that individual's living character. We must go to the other side of the life of thoughts, as it were, and then these same forces reveal themselves as working day by day from within outward, as the little child transforms an undefined physiognomy more and more into an expression of soul. They are the same forces that pass into the child's facial expressions, giving them warmth and inner fire; they are the forces that change the shape of its nose, because the nose, too, continues to change its form after birth. These same forces introduce order and purpose into the first erratic movements of a baby's limbs. Indeed, they are responsible for all that lives and moves inwardly during the entire time that physical growth continues in the young human being. When we begin to look at the life of thoughts from the point of view of anthroposophy, it is as if we are now looking into a person's face, having previously learned to know that person only from behind. Everything dead begins to live; the whole life of thought becomes alive when we start to view it internally.

In earlier times this was not consciously recognized as is now possible through anthroposophy, but it was felt and expressed in the language of myth. Today we can recognize it directly, and thus carry it into practical life. If we enter into these things in a deep and living way, therefore, we can educate the child artistically, we can make pedagogy into an art.

If you know thinking only from behind, only from its "dead" side, you will understand the child only intellectually. If you learn to know thinking from the front, from its living side, you can approach children so that you do not merely understand them, but can also enter into all of their feelings and impulses so that you pour love into all of the children's experiences.

In general, nothing that lives has survived all these things. Current civilization has only the *word* for thought; it no longer holds the *substance* that the word represents. When we speak of the science of the soul, we no longer speak of reality. We have become accustomed to using the old words, but the words have lost their substance. Language has lost its content in connection with the life of feeling, and with the life of the will—even more than with the life of thought. Feelings push their way up from the subconscious. The human being lives in them but cannot look down into the subconscious depths. And when it is done, it is done in an amateurish way through the eyes of a psychoanalyst. The psychoanalyst does not reach or find the soul element that lives and moves in the subconscious of a person's feelings. So for feelings, too, only the words remain; and this loss of substance applies even more to the will sphere. If we wanted to describe what we know about these things today, we should not speak of the human will at all, because will has become a mere word in our present civilization. When we see a person writing, for example, we can only describe how the hand begins to move, how the hand holds the pen, and how the pen moves over the paper; we are justified only in describing the external facts that are displayed in movement. These are still facts today, but the inherent will in the activity of writing is no longer experienced. It has become a mere word.

Anthroposophy's job is to restore real substance and meaning to the words of our so-called science of the soul. For this reason, anthroposophy can offer a true knowledge of the human being, whereas in our present civilization, verbosity spreads like a veil over the true facts of psychology. It is interesting to note that the late Fritz Mauthner wrote *Critique of Language* because he found that when people speak of things pertaining to soul and spirit today, they speak in mere words.[1] He pointed out that today people have only words devoid of true meaning; but he should have gone further in drawing attention to the necessity for finding again the true content in words.

From a general scientific perspective, Mauthner's *Critique of Language* is, of course, nonsensical; for I would like to know if anyone who grasps a hot iron could possibly be unable to distinguish the fact from the word. If someone

---

1. Fritz Mauthner (1849–1923), German writer, theater critic, and skeptic philosopher.

merely says the words, "The iron is hot," the iron does not burn the speaker. Only if touched does it burn. Those who stand amid life know very well how to discriminate between physical reality and the words that natural science uses to designate it—that is, assuming they haven't been completely ruined by too much theorizing.

Psychology, however, stops at this point; only words are left. And someone like Mauthner, with the best of intentions, says that we should do away with the word *soul* altogether. (Here we see something inwardly arising to the surface, which will find outer expression later.) Therefore, according to Mauthner, we should not speak of *the soul*, but coin a new abstraction to avoid the erroneous view that we are referring to a concrete reality when speaking of *the* human soul. Mauthner is perfectly correct as far as contemporary civilization is concerned. Today a new penetration into the soul's true nature is necessary, so that the word *soul* may again be filled with inner meaning.

It is indeed devastating to see people merely playing around with words when it comes to knowledge of the soul—if it can be called knowledge at all—whereas, the true nature of the soul remains untouched. As a result, people puzzle over problems, such as, whether the soul affects the body or the body affects the soul, or whether these two phenomena are parallel to each other. As far as such matters are concerned, there is no insight to be found anywhere, and therefore any discussion and argument is bound to remain abstract and arbitrary. Yet, if these things are habitually discussed only from an external viewpoint, one loses all the enthusiasm and inner warmth that the teacher, as an artist, should bring to the classroom. Parents also, by the way, should have been able to acquire these qualities simply by virtue of living in a vital culture, so they could have the right relationship with their growing children.

What we are saying is this: one pillar of the art of education is psychology, the science of the soul. But in this culture, we have no science of the soul. And even worse, we lack the honesty to admit it, because we cater to the authority of the physical sciences. So we talk about the soul without having any knowledge of it. This falsehood is carried into the most intimate recesses of human life. On the other hand, it must be said that there is undoubtedly much sincere good will among those who today speak about the ideals of education, and who supply the world so liberally with ideas of reform. There is plenty of good will, but we lack the courage to acknowledge that we must first come up with a true science of the human soul before we may so much as open our lips to speak about educational reform, about the art of education. To begin with, we must recognize that we do not have the first of the two main pillars on which we rely—that is, true insight into the life of the soul. We have the words for it, words that have been coined in far-distant antiquity, but we no longer have an experience of the living soul.

The second pillar is represented by the sum of our moral principles. If on the one hand our psychology consists of mere words, a "psychology without a psyche," so on the other hand, our moral teaching is bereft of divine inspiration. True, the old religious teachings have been preserved in the form of various traditions. But the substance of the old religious teachings lives as little in the people today as does the science of the soul, which has shriveled into words. People confess to what is handed down to them in the form of religious dogma or rituals, because it corresponds to old habits, and because, over the course of evolution, they have grown accustomed to what is offered to them. But the living substance is no longer there. So there is a psychology without a soul and ethics without real contact with the divine and spiritual world.

When people speak theoretically or want to satisfy emotional needs, they still use words that are relics of ancient moral teachings. These words were used at one time to accomplish the will of the gods; we still speak in words coined in those distant times, when humans knew that the forces working in moral life were potent forces like the forces of nature or the forces of divine beings. They knew that divine spiritual beings gave reality to these ethical impulses, to these moral forces. To this day, people express these origins in various ways, inasmuch as their daily lives are lived in the words handed down from earlier religions. But they have lost the ability to see the living divine spirituality that gives reality to their ethical impulses.

Dear friends, can people today honestly say that they understand, for example, the epistles of Saint Paul, when he says that in order not to die, human beings need to awaken to the living Christ within? Is it possible for people to feel, in the fullest sense of the word, that immoral conduct cannot possibly be associated with the moral duties of the soul, just as health and illness have to do with life and death of the body? Is there still a spiritual understanding of how the soul dies in the spirit unless it remains in touch with the moral forces of life? Do Saint Paul's words still live when he says that, unless you know that the Christ has arisen, your faith, your soul, is dead? And that when you pass through physical death your soul becomes infected by physical death, and begins to die in the spirit? Does an understanding of these things, an inner, living understanding, still exist?

Worse yet, our civilization has not the courage to admit this lack of inner, living understanding. It is satisfied with natural science, which can speak only about what is dead, but not about the living human soul. It is strictly through habit that this civilization of ours accepts what is said about the immortality of the soul and about the resurrection of the Christ on Earth. Hasn't this materialistic spirit pervaded even theology itself?

Let us look at the most modern form of theology. People have lost the insight that the Christ event stands in earthly world history as something spiritual and can be judged only on spiritual grounds; they have lost the insight that one cannot understand the resurrection with natural-scientific concepts, but only through spiritual science. Even the theologians have lost this insight. They speak only of the man Jesus and can no longer reach a living comprehension of the resurrected, living Christ; basically, they fall under Saint Paul's verdict: "Unless you know that Christ has arisen, your faith is dead."

Unless we succeed in calling to life between the ages of seven and fourteen the living Christ in the inner being of the child, with the help of the kind of pedagogy that anthroposophy describes, unless we succeed in doing this, human beings will step into later life unable to gain an understanding of the living Christ. They will have to deny Christ, unless they choose, somewhat dishonestly, to hold on to the traditional Christian beliefs, while lacking the inner means of soul to understand that Christ has risen insofar as the person experiences the resurrection, and insofar as the teacher experiences with the child the living Christ in the heart, in the soul. Christ can be awakened in the soul, and through this union with Christ, immortality can be restored to the soul.

In order that immortality be given back to the soul, there must first be a spiritual understanding of what immortality really is. One must first come to the point where one can say: When we look at nature by itself, we are faced with natural laws that teach us that our Earth will die by heat one day, that the time will come when everything on Earth will die away. But unless we have some insight into the living spirituality of the world, we are bound to believe that our moral ideas and principles will also die in the general heat; that death will befall the Earth and that everything will end up as one great cemetery.

If we do have insight into the living spirit, however, we will realize that the moral impulses welling up from the soul are received by the divine spiritual beings, just as we receive the oxygen in the air that keeps life going. Then we know that what we do in the moral sphere is received by the divine spiritual beings of the world, and consequently our soul itself is borne out into other worlds, beyond the destruction of the physical Earth.

We must be able to make this knowledge an intrinsic part of our view of life, and take it into our thinking life and into our feelings, just as today we integrate what we learn about X-rays, telephones, and electromagnetism. People believe in all these because their senses experience a direct inner connection with them. To have a true and living relation to these matters, we must experience a living connection with them; we must live with them. Otherwise, in connection with the things of the soul, we would be like the artist who knows what is beautiful and the rules for making a work of art beautiful, but who knows it in dry, abstract, intellectual concepts without being able to wield a brush, use colors, knead clay, or otherwise handle any artist's materials. If we want to find our way to the living human being, we must seek the power to do so in the living spiritual life itself. Spirituality, however, is lacking in our present civilization. And yet, spirituality has to be the second pillar on which the art of teaching rests.

Teachers today who should be artists of education confront the students with a purely natural-scientific attitude. The realm of the human soul has fallen away to become a mere collection of words; and the spiritual world, the moral world, has itself sunk to the level of a collection of ceremonies. We would begin an art of education based on science of the soul and on morality; but we are faced with a "soulless science of the soul" and an ethics devoid of the spiritual. We would speak of Christ, but to be able to speak of Him properly, it is necessary to have absorbed the quality of *soul*, something of the divine and spiritual. If we have neither, we can speak only of Jesus the man—that is, we speak only of the man who walked among people in a physical body like any other human being.

If we want to recognize the Christ and put the power of the Christ to work in schools, we need more than a science of the soul and an ethics made only of words. We need living insight into the life and work of the soul, into the working and weaving of moral forces, similar to the weaving and working of natural forces. We must know moral forces as realities, not merely a form of conventional morality. Instead of accepting them out of habit, we should see that we must live in these moral forces, for we know that unless we do so, we die in the spirit, even as we die in the body when our blood solidifies.

Such contemplations in all their liveliness must become a kind of life-capital, especially for the art of education. An enlivening and mobile force, bringing to life what is dead, needs to permeate the teacher's whole being when endeavoring to educate and teach.

Whether educated or not, people today talk about the soul in lifeless words. When speaking about the spirit today, we live only in dead words. We do not live in the living soul, and so merely splash about and hover around the child, for we have lost the key to the soul of childhood. We try to understand the child's body by engaging in all manner of experimental methods, but it remains dark and silent for us, because behind everything physical lives the spiritual. If we wish to lead the spiritual into an art and if we wish to avoid remaining with a merely intellectual conception of it, using abstract thoughts that have lost their power, then the spiritual has to be apprehended in its living manifestations.

As mentioned earlier, one hears it said everywhere that the art of teaching should be built on two main pillars—that is, on ethics and on the science of the soul. At the same time, one hears bitter doubts expressed as to how one should go about educating children. It was pointed out that, in earlier times, the child was seen as a future adult, and educated accordingly. This is true; for example, how did the Greeks educate their children? They did not really pay much attention to the life and experience of children during their childhood. Children who would obviously never grow into proper Greek adults, were simply left to die. The child as such was of no consequence; only the adult was considered important. In all their education of the young, the Greeks considered only future adults.

Today we have reached a stage in our civilization where children no longer respond unless we attend to their needs. Those with experience in such matters know what I mean. If we do not give them their due, children will resist inwardly; they do not cooperate unless the adults allow them to be themselves and do not consider them only from the adult viewpoint. This brings many problems with it concerning education. Should our education aim to satisfy the child's specific needs, or should we consider how to awaken what the child must become one day as an adult?

Such questions arise if one observes the child only from the outside, as it were—when one no longer perceives the inner human being. Certainly, we will not come near children at all if we educate them with an understanding that has arisen from experimental psychology, or with one that sees things from a viewpoint that would lead logically to experimental psychology. The inner soul being of a child is not carried outwardly on the surface so that one only needs to understand them in a way that might be sufficient for understanding an adult. Merely to understand the child, however, is not enough; we must be able to live inwardly with it. What is essentially human must have entered us directly enough that we can truly live with the child. Mere understanding of the child is completely useless.

If we can enter the child's life livingly, we are no longer faced with the contradictory alternatives of either educating the child as a child or educating the child as a potential grown-up. Then we know that, whatever we have to offer the child, we must bring it so that it accords with the child's own will; we know also that, at the same time, we are educating the future adult in the child. Do children in their inmost nature really want to be only children? If this were so, they would not play with dolls, in this way imitating the ways of the grown-up world. Nor would children experience such delight in "working" with craftsmen when there is a workshop nearby. In reality, of course, children play, but to children such imitative play is serious work.

Children truly long to develop, in their own way, the forces that adults develop. If we understand the human being and thereby also the child, we know that the child, through play, is always striving toward adulthood, except that a child will play with a doll instead of a living baby. We also know that children experience the greatest joy when, as part of what we bring them in education, we educate the future adults in them. This must be done properly, not in the dry and prosaic way that reflects our frequent attitude toward work as an irksome and troublesome task, but so that work itself becomes second nature to the human being. In the eyes of a child, work thus assumes the same quality as its own earnest and serious play.

When we have a living understanding of this way of educating—and not merely an abstract idea of it—we are no longer beset by doubt about whether we should educate the grown-up person in the child, or the child as such. We then see in the child the seed of adulthood, but we do not address this seed in the way we would address an adult. We speak in the child's own language. And so, unless we can come very close to the nature of the young human being, wherever we turn we find ideas that are nothing but empty words. It is the task of anthroposophy to lead people away from, and beyond, these empty words.

Today, there is an ongoing conflict between materialism and a spiritual view of the world. You hear people say that we must overcome materialism, we must come back again to a spiritual viewpoint. But for anthroposophy, the concept of matter, in the form that haunts the thoughts of people today like a ghost, has lost all meaning; because, if one comes to know matter as it really is, it begins to grow transparent and dissolves into spirit, to speak pictorially. If one understands matter properly, it becomes transformed into spirit. And if one understands spirit properly, it becomes transformed into matter before the eye of the soul, so that matter becomes the outward revelation of spirit in its creative power.

The words *matter* and *spirit*, used in a one-sided way, no longer have any meaning. If we begin to speak from the standpoint of this deeper perception, however, we may still talk about spirit and matter; after all, these words have been coined, but we use them in a very different way. When we say the words *matter* or *material substance*, we give them yet another coloring with our feeling if we have behind us the anthroposophical knowledge I have just described. The word *matter* or *material* takes on another, more hidden timbre, and it is this hidden timbre that works upon the child and not the content of the word *matter*.

Reflect for a moment about how much human understanding and feeling live in the word when used with full comprehension! Suppose someone had felt, as Fritz Mauthner did, that we have no more than words for what refers to the soul, and that it would be truer, in fact, not to speak any longer of *the soul (Seele)*, but to speak of *a generic soul (Geseel)*. This may raise a smile. But suppose we were to carry this same attitude into the sphere of the religious and the ethical, into the moral sphere, where our accomplishments and activity take effect— suppose that, out of the same feeling, someone were to make up the appropriate word in this sphere; what would we get then? *Ado (Getue)* [rather than *Tue*, or "to do"]. As you see, I have formed the words *Geseel* and *Getue* according to the same syntactical principle. *Geseel* will at most produce a smile; *Getue* will be felt to be an outrageous word, for if all one's action and conduct were to become nothing but abstract ado (*Getue*), this word would indeed be annoying. This is not due to the content of the word, however, but arises from what we feel when the word is spoken. The experience in our feeling is quite different according to whether we are coining words that have to do with the soul nature—*Geseel*, for example—or whether we are coining words to indicate what brings us into the external world, what brings us to where our actions themselves become events in nature. If one uses the word *Getue* in this context, it will arouse indignation.

Consider how indifferently words are now used, one next to another, as it were, and one even running into one another. We speak in the same neutral way of matter, spirit, and body; of soul or of the human brain; or again, of the limbs, and so on. The ideal of natural-scientific knowledge seems to be that we should express everything neutrally without letting any human element enter into our speech, into our naming of things.

But if we no longer pour the human element into our words, they die. The abstract words of natural science die unless we infuse them with our human participation. In physics we speak, for example, of the theory of impact. At best, we write down a mathematical equation, which we don't understand when we speak of *impact* without the living sensation experienced when we ourselves push or hit something. Words can only be translated into life if we bring human beings back into our culture.

This is what anthroposophy wishes to do—restore the human element into our civilization. Things are still all right as long as we go through life in a lazy, indifferent way, simply allowing externals run their course by means of technology, the child of our wonderfully advanced physical sciences. But if we move into the spheres where one person has to help a fellow human being, as physician, teacher, or educator, then it becomes a different matter. Then we feel the need for a real, living and consciously assumed knowledge of the human being that is revealed in the art of teaching. If we talk about the need for this knowledge to fulfill the still unconscious or subconscious demands of present-day education, it is not due to any wilfulness on our part, but to a necessity of our civilization.

However many organizations may be founded to bring about educational reforms, they will be of no avail unless we first have groups of men and women ready to work at rediscovering a living knowledge of the human being—that is, a science of the soul that really has a soul and a teaching of morality that really springs from the divine and the spiritual.

Such groups must lead the way. Others may then follow that would build again on the two main pillars supporting the edifice that still needs to be built out of a true science of the soul and a true ethics—a science of the soul that doesn't merely talk in words and an ethics that knows how human moral conduct is anchored in the divine spiritual worlds. Then we shall have teachers and educators who work artistically and are thus able to at least approach the very soul of the child in whatever they say and do, even by the invisible workings of their mere presence on the child. They will find the way back to the human soul. And when they set out to educate the child ethically, they will know that they are integrating the child into a divine and spiritual world order. They will be working out of the super-sensible element, both in a true psychology and in a true spiri-tuality—that is, from genuine knowledge of the human soul; and they will introduce what belongs to the realm of the super-sensible into a true spiritual life.

These things will serve as genuine supporting pillars for the art of education. They have to be explored, and anthroposophy seeks to do this. That is why we have an anthroposophical method of education, not from personal desire or opinion, but because of the need of the times in which we live.

8

Waldorf Pedagogy

First of all, I would like to apologize for being unable to talk to you in your native language. Since this is not possible, I will speak in German, which will then be translated for you.

The methods of the Waldorf school, which I have been asked to speak about, owe their existence to the merging of two streams in cultural and spiritual life. The school was founded in Germany during the restless and disturbed times following the war, when efforts were made to create new conditions in the social realm. It all began with the ideas of the industrialist Emil Molt, who wished to begin a school for the children of the employees in his factory. This school was to offer an education that would enable the students to grow eventually into adults, well equipped to participate in social life as rational and full human beings, based on the idea that social change should not be at the mercy of political agitators. This constituted the primary element at first; the other came later.

Emil Molt had been a long-standing member of the anthroposophical movement, which is trying to reintroduce spiritual knowledge into the social life of the present times, a spiritual knowledge equally well grounded in the realities of human truths as the natural sciences, which have reached outstanding prominence and made great achievements during the last few centuries. Mister Molt asked me, in my capacity as the leader of the anthroposophical movement, to introduce pedagogical and practical methods into this new Waldorf school.

The school's approach is not the product of the current movements for educational reform; it is based instead on a pedagogy drawing on deep concrete knowledge of the human being.

Over the course of our civilization we have gradually lost true knowledge of the human being. We turn our eyes increasingly to external nature and see only the physical and natural foundation of the human being. Certainly, this natural physical foundation must not be considered unimportant in the field of education; nevertheless, the human being consists of body, soul, and spirit, and a real knowledge of the human being can be achieved only when spirit, soul, and body are recognized equally.

The principles of Waldorf pedagogy do not depend in any way on local conditions, because this pedagogy is based on a knowledge of the human being, including that of the growing human being, the child. From this point of view it is immaterial whether one thinks of rural or city schools, of boarding schools or of day schools. Because Waldorf schools are based strictly on pedagogical and pragmatic principles, they can meet and adapt to any possible external social conditions.

Furthermore, the Waldorf school is a school for all types of children. Although at first it was opened for the children of Mister Molt's factory, today, children from all social classes and backgrounds have been accepted there, because pedagogical and practical impulses based on real knowledge of the human being are universally human; they are international in character and relevant for all classes and races of humanity.

Here I do not want to give a detailed account of the Waldorf curriculum—there is too little time for that. In general, the school is built not so much on a fixed program as on direct daily practice and immediate contact with the children according to their character, therefore, I can give only brief indications of the main principles that underlie the Waldorf school, and I must ask you to keep this in mind.

To know the human being means, above all, to have more than the usual knowledge about how the human being's life goes through different life stages. Although educational theories have generally considered these stages more or less, in Waldorf pedagogy they are considered in full.

In this context I must emphasize that around the child's seventh year—at the change of teeth—a complete transformation takes place, a complete metamorphosis in the life of the child. When the second teeth begin to appear, the child becomes an altogether different being. Where does this transformation originate? With the arrival of the seventh year, the forces that had been the forces for physical growth, working in the child's breathing and blood circulation and building the organism in its nutritive and growth activity, are now released. While leaving a remainder behind to carry on with this organic task, these forces themselves go through an important transformation as they enter the child's metamorphosing soul life.

Recently, many psychological studies have examined how the soul works into the child's physical organism. A proper science of the spirit does not float around in a mystical fog, but observes life and the world with clear perception, based on direct experience. Thus, spiritual science does not pose abstract questions about how soul and body are related, but asks instead through direct experience, while observing life itself, as clearly as external scientific experiments are observed.

One finds, therefore, that between birth and the change of teeth, the child's soul forces manifest as organic forces working in the child's physical body. These same forces, in a somewhat emancipated form, manifest purely in the soul realm (the child's thinking and memory) in the following period between the change of teeth and puberty. The teacher's first prerequisite, which has to become thoroughly integrated into attitude and character, is to sharpen the perception of the metamorphosis in human life that takes place around the age of seven and, further, to be conscious of the immense metamorphosis that occurs at puberty, at fourteen or fifteen.

If the growing child is approached with this viewpoint, one fact looms very large in one's knowledge—that, until the age of seven, every child is a universal sense organ that relates as an organism to the surroundings, just as the eyes or ears relate as sense organs to the external world. Each sense organ can receive impressions from its surroundings and reflect them pictorially. Until the seventh year, the child inwardly pulsates with intense elemental forces. Impressions are received from the surroundings as if the child's whole being were one large sense organ. The child is entirely an imitating being.

When studying the child, one finds that, until the seventh year, the physical organization is directly affected by external impressions, and later on this relationship is spiritualized and transformed into a religious relationship. We understand the child up to the change of teeth only when we perceive the forces and impulses that, based on the physical and soul organization, turn the child entirely into *homo religiosus*. Consequently it is incumbent on those who live close to the young child to act according to this particular situation. When we are in the presence of a young child, we have to act only in ways that may be safely imitated. For example, if a child is suspected of stealing, facts may be discovered that I can illustrate with a particular case: Parents once approached me in a state of agitation to tell me that their young boy had stolen. I immediately told them that one would have to investigate properly whether this was really the case. What had the boy done? He had spent money which he had taken from his mother's cupboard. He had bought sweets with it and shared them with other children. He had even performed a sociable deed in the process! Every day he had seen his mother taking money from a certain place before she went shopping. He could see only what was right in his mother's action, and so he imitated her. The child simply imitated his mother and was not a thief.

We must make sure that the child can safely imitate whatever happens in the surroundings. This includes—and this is important—sentiments and feelings, even one's thoughts. The best educators of children under the age of seven do not just outwardly act in a way that is all right for the child to imitate—they do not even allow themselves any emotions or feelings, not even thoughts, other than what the child may imitate without being harmed.

One has to be able to observe properly how the entire process of education affects the child from the spiritual point of view. During the first seven years of life, everything that happens around the child affects the physical organization of that child. We must be able to perceive the effects of people's activity in front of children. Let's imagine, for example, that someone is prone to outbursts of a violent temper. Consequently, a child near that person is frequently subjected to the actions of a violent temperament and experiences shocks caused by an aggressive nature. These shocks affect not only the soul of the child, but also the breathing and blood circulation, as well as the vascular system.

If one knows human nature completely and observes not just particular ages but the entire course of life from birth to death, one also knows that anything that affects the vascular system, the blood circulation, and the intimate processes of breathing through physical and spiritual causes and impressions coming from the external world, will manifest in a person's organization until the fortieth and fiftieth year of life. A child who is tossed about by confusing impressions will suffer from an unreliable coordination of breathing and blood circulation. We are not necessarily talking about obvious medical problems, but of subtle effects in the blood circulatory system, which must be recognized by those who wish to educate children.

The seventh year brings the change of teeth, which represents the end of a chapter, since we change our teeth only once in a lifetime. The forces that led to the second dentition are now liberated for later life, and now enter the mind and soul of the human being; for during the time of elementary schooling, the forces that had previously been involved in plastically shaping the child's organism can now be seen working musically, so to speak, in the organism until puberty. Until the age of seven, the head organization works on the rest of the human organism. The human head is the great sculptor that forms the vascular system and the blood circulation, and so on. From the ages of seven to fifteen, the rhythmic system in the widest sense becomes the leading system of the human organism. If we can give rhythm and measure to this rhythmic system in our lessons and in our way of teaching—*measure* in the musical sense—as well as of giving a general musical element through the way we conduct our teaching in all lessons, then we meet the essential demands of human nature at this stage of life.

Education from the change of teeth until puberty should appeal primarily to the artistic aspect in children. An artistic element definitely pervades the Waldorf curriculum from the students' seventh to fourteenth years. Children are guided pictorially in every respect. Thus, the letters of the alphabet are not taught abstractly. There is no human relationship to the abstract symbols that have become letters in our civilization.

Written symbols are abstractions to children. We allow the letters to evolve from pictures. At first, we let our young students paint and draw, and only then do we evolve the forms of the letters from the drawings and paintings that flowed directly from their human nature. Only after the child's whole organism—body, soul, and spirit—has become fully immersed in writing, through an artistic activity, only then do we go over to another activity, one involving only a part of the human being. Only then do we go to reading, because reading does not involve the complete human being, but only a part, whereas writing is evolved from the entire human organization. If one proceeds this way, one has treated the human individual according to the realities of body, soul, and spirit. If one's teaching is arranged so that the artistic element can flow through the children, so that in whatever the teachers do they become artists in their work, something rather remarkable can be observed.

As you know, much thought has gone into the question of avoiding exhaustion in students during lessons. Diagrams have been constructed to show which mental or physical activities tire students most. In Waldorf schools, on the other hand, we appeal to the particular human system that never tires at all. The human being tires in the head through thinking, and also gets tired when doing physical work—when using will forces in performing limb movements. But the rhythmic system, with its breathing and heart system (the basis of every artistic activity) always works, whether one is asleep or awake, whether tired or fresh, because the rhythmic system has a particular way of working from birth until death. The healthiest educational system, therefore, appeals to the human rhythmic system, which never tires.

You can see, therefore, that all teaching, all education, in order to be faithful to a fundamental knowledge of the human being, must be based on the rhythmic system, must appeal to the students' rhythmic forces. By bringing flexibility and music into all teaching, always beginning with the pictorial, rhythmical, melodious, and a generally musical element, one may notice something rather surprising—that, as the child progresses as a result of artistic activities, a powerful need is expressed in relation to what was developed through this pictorial and musical understanding of the world. It becomes evident that this artistic approach is too rich for permanent inner satisfaction. Soon—by the age of ten or eleven—students feel the need for a more direct approach and for simplification, because the artistic realm becomes too rich for their continued inner enjoyment. The desire for simplification becomes a natural and elementary need in the students.

Only when this process begins, has the right moment arrived for making the transition from an artistic approach to a more intellectual one. Only after the child has been allowed to experience artistic wealth is it possible to introduce the relative poverty of the intellectual element without the risk of disturbing the child's physical and soul development. This is why we extract the intellectual from the artistic qualities.

On the other hand, if one lets the children perform artistic movements, if one has them move their limbs musically, as in eurythmy (which is being performed here in Ilkley), if one encourages a sculptural, formative activity in the child, as well as musical movements that take hold of the entire body, then a remarkable hunger makes itself felt in the child—a spiritual, soulful, and bodily hunger. At this stage the child's whole organization demands specific physical exercises, a specific physical hygiene, because a physical hygiene is healthy for the development of the human organism only when a mysterious kind of hunger is felt for the kinds of movements performed in gymnastics. In other words, the students' feeling of a need for intellectual pursuit and for will activities arises from artistic development.

As a result of this, we have education that does not aim to develop only a particular part of human nature, but aims to develop the whole human being. We are given the possibility, for example, to train the child's memory for the benefit of the physical organization. In this context, I would like to say something that sounds paradoxical today, but will be fully accepted by physiology in the future: Everything that works spiritually in the child affects the physical organization at the same time, and even enters the corporeality, the physical organism itself. For example, we might see people today who, around their fiftieth year, begin to suffer from metabolic diseases, such as rheumatism. If, as educators, we do not limit our observations of students only to the age of childhood, but recognize that childhood is like a seedbed for all of life to come—like the seed in the life of the plant—then one also recognizes that, when we strain the child's powers of memory, the effect will bear right through the organism, so that in the forties or fifties metabolic illnesses will appear that the physical organization can no longer correct.

When I suggest these interconnections, you may believe me that in the Waldorf school we make every effort to ensure that the soul and spiritual aspect will have a beneficial effect on the student's physical constitution. Every lesson is looked at from the hygienic viewpoint because we can see how spirit continues to affect the human organism. Because our pedagogy and our methods rest on our insight into the human being, we are in a position to create our curriculum and our educational goals for the various ages from direct observation of the growing child. We take up only what the child reveals as necessary. Our pedagogy is completely based on applied knowledge of the human being.

This approach makes us confident that our education is accomplished not just from the perspective of childhood, but also from the viewpoint of the entire earthly life of any child in our care. There are people who, for example, believe that one should teach a child only what can be understood through the child's own observation; now, from a different perspective, this may be a valid opinion, but those who make such a statement ignore the value that the following situation has for life.

Between the age of seven and puberty it is most beneficial for students if their attitude toward the teacher results from a natural authority. Just as, until the age of seven, the ruling principle is imitation, so also between seven and fourteen the ruling principle is the teacher's authority. At this stage, much of what is as still beyond the student's comprehension is accepted in the soul simply through trust in the teacher's authority, through a respect and an attitude of love toward the teacher. This kind of love is one of the most important educational factors.

It is important to know that, at the age of thirty or forty, one may remember something that one had accepted at the age of eight or nine on the strength of a beloved teacher's authority. Now, as it rises up to the surface again in the soul, it permeates one's adult consciousness. Through one's powers, which have matured in the meantime, one begins to understand what was accepted at the age of eight or nine based merely on a beloved teacher's authority. When such a thing happens, it is a source of human rejuvenation. It really revitalizes the entire human being in later life if, after decades, one eventually understands what one had accepted previously through a natural feeling of authority. This is another example of the need to consider the entire vista of human life and not only what is perceptible in a one-sided way in the present condition.

I would like to give another example from a moral perspective. If a child's inherent religious feelings are nourished during religious education—feelings that live naturally in every child—the following observation can be made: Are there not people who, having reached a certain age, merely by their presence create a mood of blessing in those around them? We have all experienced how such a person enters a gathering. It is not the words of wisdom such people may speak that radiate this effect of blessing; their presence, tone of voice, and gestures are enough to create a mood of blessing in those around them. Such persons can teach us when we look back to their childhood days, at how they achieved this ability to bring grace and blessing to those around them. In childhood they respected a loved authority with almost religious veneration. No one in old age can be a blessing who has not learned in childhood to look up in loving veneration to a revered person of authority. I would like to express this symbolically in this way: If one wishes to be able in later life to lift one's hands in blessing, one must have learned to fold them in prayer during childhood. Symbolically, the folded hands of prayer during childhood lead to the blessing hands of old age.

At all times and everywhere we must consider the whole human being. During childhood we plant the seeds for an inner religious sense of morality and for an adulthood strong enough to meet life's demands. This can be done when one tries to build a pedagogy from full knowledge of the human being, knowledge that is the result of observation, from birth to the grave. Striving toward educational renewal has become prominent and intensive in our time because the greatest social question is really a question of education.

I have spoken only briefly here about the deep inner attitude that, permeated with a universal love for humanity, glows throughout Waldorf pedagogy. Therefore, however weak and imperfect our attempts may be, we nevertheless cherish the hope that an education based on a fuller knowledge of the human being can, at the same time, be an education for all of humanity in the best sense. To work at school through observation of human life may be the best way also to work toward the good of life everywhere. This will certainly be the fundamental question inherent in most of the striving for educational reform in our time.

9

Anthroposophy and Education

THE HAGUE — NOVEMBER 14, 1923

In diverse quarters today, people speak of the need for an answer to certain educational questions thus far unanswered. The many endeavors in modern education clearly show this. What I am hoping to convey to you today, at the request of this country's Anthroposophical Society, is not mere theoretical knowledge. The practical application of spiritual-scientific knowledge that comes from the anthroposophical viewpoint of the human being has already demonstrated its value—at least to a certain extent.

In 1919 Emil Molt took the first steps to open a free school, and he asked me to take care of the practical matters and direction of the school. Thus, the spiritual-scientific knowledge of the human being and the world, which it is my task to represent, became naturally the basis of the education practiced in this school. The school has existed since 1919 and currently offers twelve grades. Students who entered the twelfth grade this summer will take their final exams next year so they can enter a university or other places of higher education. The school offers everything pertaining to the education of children from the elementary school age (that is, after the age of six) until the boys and girls begin higher education.

This school's practices, which are the outcome of a spiritual-scientific worldview, was never intended to revolutionize any previous achievements in the field of practical education. Our goal is not to think up new radical methods, such as those tried in special rural boarding schools, where the creation of very particular conditions was believed necessary before teaching could even begin. Our aim is to continue along the educational paths already marked by enlightened educators at the beginning of the twentieth century. This we attempt not only on the basis of human knowledge during the various stages of earthly development, but out of insight into the whole of human nature in the widest and most comprehensive way possible. This insight includes not only the various physical happenings of earthly life between birth and death, but also what lives and manifests during life as the eternally divine in the human being. It is important to us that we add to what has already been achieved by educational reformers, and also that we offer what can be contributed from a wider, spiritual viewpoint. Furthermore, there is no intention of putting utopian educational ideas into the world—something that, as a rule, is far easier to do than creating something based fully on practical reality. Our aim is to achieve the best possible results under any given circumstances.

Achieving this goal means that the actual conditions one faces, whether urban or rural, must serve as a foundation for the human being that results from a genuine and true art of education, so that students can eventually find a way into current and future social and professional life situations, which will certainly become increasingly complex. This is why Waldorf education offers an education that is strictly practical and methodical, meaning that, essentially, its program can be accomplished in any type of school, provided that the fundamental conditions can be created. So far, events have shown that we have made at least some progress in this direction.

We opened our school under auspicious circumstances. Initially, the manufacturer Emil Molt began it for the children of the workers in his factory. There was, of course, no difficulty in enrolling them. Also, we received children whose parents were interested in the anthroposophical point of view. Still, we began with only one hundred and thirty students. Today, four years later, after the school has grown from eight to twelve grades, we have almost eight hundred students and a staff of over forty teachers. Here in Holland, there have recently been efforts to open a similar small school—but more on that later. There is some hope that the methods used in Stuttgart will also prove worthwhile in Holland. Steps are also being taken in Switzerland to begin such a school, and in England a committee has been formed to start a Waldorf school.

After these introductory remarks I would like to speak about the meaning of Waldorf pedagogy. It is based on a penetrating knowledge of the human being, and on the teachers' ability, with the help of special preparation and training, to perceive the development and unfolding of their students' individualities, week by week, month by month, and year by year. From this point of view, the question of Waldorf education has to be seen, primarily, as a question of teacher training. I will try to outline in sketchy and unavoidably abstract form what can be done on the basis of such knowledge of the human being. This abstract form, however, can only be a description. It is important that what is said becomes flesh and blood, so to speak, in the teachers and that this deepened knowledge of the human being arises from practice and not from theory, and thus becomes applicable in a school.

When we observe the growing child, we can easily overlook the significance of changes connected with three fundamental life stages. We may notice various changes during a child's development, but usually we fail to comprehend their deeper significance. We can distinguish three fundamental stages of human development until about the twentieth year, when formal education ends, or makes way for more specialized education. The first period, which is of a homogeneous nature, begins at birth and ends with the change of teeth around the seventh year. The second life stage begins at the time of the second dentition and ends at puberty. During the third stage, we are concerned with sexually mature young people who nowadays often tend to feel more mature than we can actually treat them if we want to educate them properly. This stage lasts until around the twenty-first year.

Let's look more closely at the child's first period of life. To the unbiased observer, a child at this stage is entirely an imitating being, right into the most intimate fibers of the spirit, soul, and physical being; and above all, the child at this stage is a being of will. One will notice that the child becomes, during development, increasingly open to impressions that come from the environment, and pays more and more attention to external things and happenings. But it is easy to deceive oneself in believing that the child's increasing attentiveness to the external world is due to an awakening of a conceptual life, something that, at such an early age, is not true at all. At no other time in all of life will the human being, due to inborn instinct and drive, want to be freer and more independent of the conceptual realm than during these early years before the change of teeth. During these years the child really wants to repel everything connected with conceptual life in order to freely follow the inclinations of inner nature. The child's will, on the other hand, tends to merge with the surroundings, to the point where the will manifests physically. Nothing seems more obvious than a child's tendency to imitate exactly through limb movements the habitual gestures or postures of surrounding adults. This is because the child feels an overwhelming urge to continue in the will sphere what is happening in the environment, right down to fidgeting. In this sense, the child is entirely a being of will. This is true also of the child's sense perception. We can easily see that the child at that age is a being of will, even in sense perceptions—something that we must learn to see in order to become competent educators. Allow me to give some details:

Among the various sense perceptions are our perceptions of color. Very few people notice that there are really three different elements living in color perception. As a rule one speaks of "yellow" or "blue" as a color perception, but the fact that there are three elements to such a perception usually escapes notice. First, human will is engaged in our relationship to color. Let's stick with the example of yellow and blue. If we are sufficiently free from psychological bias, we soon notice that the color yellow works on us not only as a perception in the narrower sense of the word, but also affects our will. It stimulates the will to become active in an outward direction. This is where some very interesting psychological observations could be made. One could detect, for instance, how a yellow background, such as in a hall, stimulates an inclination to become outwardly active, especially if the yellow shimmers with a slightly reddish tint. If, however, we are surrounded by a blue background, we find that the stimulus on the will is directed inward, that it tends to create a pleasing and comforting mood, or feelings of humility, thus exerting a tendency toward inner activity. In this case too, interesting observations can be made, for example, that the impression created by blue is related to specific glandular secretions, so that in this case the will is an impulse stimulated by blue and directed inward.

A second element in our investigation of the effects of color perception may be the observation of the feelings stimulated by the color. A yellow or reddish-yellow color gives an impression of warmth; we have a sensation of warmth. A blue or blue-violet color creates an impression of coolness. To the same degree that the blue becomes more red, it also feels warmer. These examples, then, show the impressions of yellow and blue on the life of feeling. Only the third response represents what we could consider the *idea* of yellow or blue. But in this last element of our mental imagery, the elements of will and feeling also play a part.

If we now consider the education of children from the perspective of an unbiased knowledge of the human being, we find that the will impulses of children are developed first through color experiences. Young children adapt their physical movements according to yellow's outward-directed stimulation or with blue's inward-directed effect. This fundamental trend continues until a child loses the first teeth. Naturally, feelings and perceptions always play a part as well in response to color, but during this first life stage the effect of color on the will always predominates.

During the second life stage—from the second dentition to puberty—the experience of esthetic feelings created by color is superimposed over the existing will impulse. Thus, we can see two things: With the change of teeth, something like a calming effect in relation to color stimulation, or in other words, an inner calming from the viewpoint of the child's innate desire to "touch" color. During the time between the change of teeth and puberty, a special appreciation for warm and cold qualities in color comes into being. Finally, a more detached and prosaic relationship to the concepts *yellow* or *blue* begins only with the beginning of puberty.

What thus manifests in color perception is present also in the human being as a whole. One could say that, until the second dentition, the child has a kind of natural religious relationship of complete devotion to the surroundings. The child allows what is living in the environment to live within. Hence, we succeed best at educating (if we can call raising children during these early years "education") when we base all our guidance on the child's inborn tendency to imitate—that is, on the child's own inward experience of empathy with the surroundings. These influences include the most imponderable impulses of human life. For example, if a child's father displays a violent temper and cannot control his outbursts, the child will be markedly affected by such a situation. The fits of temper themselves are of little significance, because the child cannot understand these; but the actions, and even the gestures, of the angry person are significant. During these early years the child's entire body acts as one universal sense organ. In the child's own movements and expressions of will, the body lives out by imitating what is expressed in the movements and actions of such a father. Everything within the still impressionable and pliable body of such a child unfolds through the effects of such experiences. Blood circulation and the nerve organization, based on the conditions of the child's soul and spirit, are under this influence; they adjust to outside influences and impacts, forming inner habits. What thus becomes a child's inner disposition through the principle of imitation, remains as inner constitution for the rest of the person's life. Later in life, the blood circulation will be affected by such outwardly perceived impressions, transformed into forces of will during this most delicate stage of childhood. This must be considered in both a physical sense and its soul-aspect.

In this context, I always feel tempted to mention the example of a little boy who, at the age of four or five, was supposed to have committed what at a later stage could be called "stealing." He had taken money from one of his mother's drawers. He had not even used it for himself, but had bought sweets with it that he shared with his playmates. His father asked me what he should do with his boy, who had "stolen" money! I replied: "Of course one has to note such an act. But the boy has not stolen, because at his age the concept of stealing does not yet exist for him." In fact, the boy had repeatedly seen his mother taking money out of the drawer, and he simply imitated her. His behavior represents a perfectly normal attempt to imitate. The concept of thieving does not yet play any part in a child of this age.

One has to be conscious not to do anything in front of the child that should not be imitated; in all one does, this principle of imitation has to be considered. Whatever one wants the child to do, the example must be set, which the child will naturally copy. Consequently, one should not assign young children specially contrived occupations, as is frequently done in kindergartens; if this must be done, the teachers should be engaged in the same activities, so that the child's interest is stimulated to copy the adult.

Imitation is the principle of a healthy education up to the change of teeth. Everything has to stimulate the child's will, because the will is still entirely woven into the child's physical body and has the quality of an almost religious surrender to the environment. This manifests everywhere, in all situations.

With the change of teeth, this attitude of surrender to the environment transforms into a childlike esthetic, artistic surrender. I should like to describe this by saying that the child's natural religious impulse toward other human beings, and toward what we understand as nature, transforms into an artistic element, which has to be met with imagination and feeling. Consequently, for the second life period, the only appropriate approach to the child is artistic. The teacher and educator of children in the primary grades must be especially careful to permeate everything done during this period with an artistic quality. In this respect, new educational approaches are needed that pay particular attention to carrying these new methods into practical daily life.

I don't expect the following to create much antagonism, since so many others have expressed similar opinions. I have heard it said more often than I care to mention that the teaching profession tends to make its members pedantic. And yet, for the years between seven and fourteen, nothing is more poisonous for the child than pedantry. On the other hand, nothing is more beneficial than a teacher's artistic sense, carried by natural inner enthusiasm to encounter the child. Each activity proposed to children, each word spoken in their presence, must be rooted, not in pedantry, and not in some theoretical construct, but in artistic enthusiasm, so that the children respond with inner joy and satisfaction at being shaped by a divine natural process arising from the center of human life.

If teachers understand how to work with their students out of such a mood, they practice the only living way of teaching. And something must flow into their teaching that I can only briefly sketch here. I am speaking of a quality that addresses partly the teachers' understanding and partly their willingness to take the time in their work, but mainly their general attitude. Knowledge of the human being has to become second nature to teachers, a part of their very being, just as the ability to handle paints and brushes has to be part of a painter's general makeup, or the use of sculpting tools natural to a sculptor. In the teacher's case, however, this ability has to be taken much more earnestly, almost religiously, because in education we are confronted with the greatest work of art we will ever encounter in life—which it would be almost sacrilegious to refer to as merely a work of art. As teachers, we are called on to help in this divine creation. It is this inner mood of reverence in the teacher that is important. Through such a mood, one finds ways to create a more and more enlivening relationship with the children.

Remember, at school young students must grow into something that is initially alien to their nature. As an example, let's take writing, which is based on letters that are no longer experienced esthetically, but are strung together to make words and sentences. Our contemporary writing developed from something very different, from picture writing. But the ancient picture writing still had a living connection with what it expressed, just as the written content retained a living relationship with its meaning. Today we need learned studies to trace back the little "goblin," which we designate as the letter *a*, to the moment when what was to be expressed through the insertion of this letter into one or the other word was inwardly experienced. And yet this *a* is nothing but an expression of a feeling of sudden surprise and wonder. Each letter has its origin in the realm of feeling, but those feelings are now lost. Today, letters are abstractions.

If one has unbiased insight into the child's mind, one knows how terribly alien the abstractions are that the child is supposed to learn at a delicate age, written meaning that once had living links with life, but now totally bereft of its earlier associations as used in the adult world today.

As a result, we in the Waldorf school have endeavored to coax writing out of the activity of painting and drawing. We teach writing before we teach reading. To begin with, we do not let the children approach letters directly at all. For example, we allow the child to experience the activity of painting—for example, the painting of a fish—however primitive the efforts may be. So the child has painted a fish. Then we make the child aware of the sound that the thing painted on paper makes when pronounced as a word; we make the child aware that what was painted is pronounced "fish." It is now an easy and obvious step to transform the shape of the fish into the sound of the first letter of the word *F-ish*. With the letter *F*, this actually represents its historical origin. However, this is not the point; the important thing is that, from the painted form of a picture, we lead to the appropriate letter.

The activity of painting is naturally connected with the human being. In this way we enable children to assimilate letters through their own experience of outer realities. This necessitates an artistic sense. It also forces one to overcome a certain easygoing attitude, because if you could see Waldorf children using their brushes and paints, you would soon realize that, from the teacher's perspective, a measure of personal discomfort is inevitable in the use of this method! Again and again the teacher has to clean up after the children, and this demands a certain devotion. Yet, such minor problems are overcome more quickly than one might assume. It is noteworthy to see how much even young children gain artistic sensibility during such activities. They soon realize the difference between "smearing" paint onto paper somewhat haphazardly, and achieving the luminous quality of watercolor needed to create the desired effects. This difference, which may appear downright "occult" to many adults, soon becomes very real to the child, and such a fertile mind and soul experience is an added bonus in this introduction to writing.

On the other hand, teaching children to write this way is bound to take more time. Learning to write a little later, however, is not a disadvantage. We all suffer because, as children, we were taught writing abstractly and too early. There would be no greater blessing for humanity than for its members to make the transition to the abstract letters of the alphabet as late as the age of nine or ten, having previously derived them from a living painterly approach.

When learning to write, the whole human being is occupied. One has to make an effort to move the arms in the right way, but at the same time one feels this activity of the arms and hands connected with one's whole being. It therefore offers a beautiful transition, from the stage when the child lives more in the will element, to the second stage when the element of feeling predominates. While learning to read, the child engages primarily the organs used to perceive the form of the letters, but the child's whole being is not fully involved. For this reason, we endeavor to evolve reading from writing. A similar approach is applied for everything the child has to learn.

The important point is for the teacher to read what needs to be done in teaching within the child's own nature. This sentence is symptomatic of all Waldorf pedagogy. As long as the teacher teaches reading in harmony with the child's nature, there is no point in stressing the advantages of one or another method. What matters is that teachers be capable of perceiving what needs to be drawn out of the child. Whatever we need in later life always evolves from what was planted in our childhood.

To sense what wants to flow out of the inner being of the child, to develop empathy with the child between the ages of seven and fourteen, are the things that give children the right footing later in life. In this context, it is especially important to develop mobile concepts in students of that age. Flexible concepts based on the life of feeling cannot be developed properly if teachers limit their subject to include only what a child already understands. It certainly appears to make sense to plead that one should avoid teaching a subject that a child cannot yet comprehend. It all sounds plausible.

On the other hand, one could be driven to despair by textbooks delineating specific methods, and by books intended to show teachers what subject to teach in their object lessons and how to do it so that students are not instructed in anything beyond their present comprehension. The substance of such books is often full of trivialities and banalities; they fail to allow that, at this age, children can glimpse in their own souls what is not sense perceptible at all outwardly, such as moral and other impulses in life. Those who advocate these observational methods do not recognize that one educates not just on the basis of what can be observed at the child's present stage, but on the basis of what will develop out of childhood for the whole of future life.

It is a fact that, whenever a child of seven or eight feels natural reverence and respect for a teacher who is seen as the gateway into the world (instinctively of course, as is appropriate to this age), such a child can rise inwardly and find support in the experience of a justified authority—not just in what the teacher says, but in the way the teacher acts, by example. This stage is very different from the previous one, when the principle of imitation is the guiding factor until the change of teeth. The early imitative attitude in the child transforms later into inner life forces. At this second stage of life, nothing is more important than the child's acceptance of truths out of trust for the teacher, because the child who has a proper sense of authority will accept the teacher's words could only be the truth. Truth has to dawn upon the child in a roundabout way—through the adult first. Likewise, appreciation for what is beautiful and good also has to evolve from the teachers' attitudes.

At this stage of life, the world must meet the child in the form of obvious authority. Certainly you will not misunderstand that, having thirty years ago written *Intuitive Thinking as a Spiritual Path: A Philosophy of Freedom*, I am speaking against human freedom. But even the most liberated of individuals should have experienced in childhood the infinitely beneficial effects of being able to look up to the authority of an educator as a matter of course—to have experienced through this respect for authority the gateway to truth, beauty, and goodness in the world. All this can be observed, week by week and month by month.

The child becomes the book where one reads what is needed. In this way one develops a profound sense for what to do with the child, for example, at any significant moment in the child's life. One such moment is between the ninth and tenth years. Anyone who has become a natural authority for the child will inevitably find, through observing the child, that, between nine and ten, a significant change occurs that can be expressed in many ways. At this point in development, children need something fairly specific, but are not at all conscious of what they need.

Here is the situation: Until this stage children have experienced the authority of their educators entirely unconsciously and instinctively. Now more is required; the students now want to feel reassured that their feeling toward the authority of the teachers is fully justified, given their more mature and critical gift of observation. If at this point a teacher succeeds in keeping the aura of natural authority alive, then later in life, perhaps in the child's forty-fifth or fiftieth year, there will be times when memories reemerge. Therefore, what was accepted at one time on trust during childhood days, maybe at the age of eight or nine, is considered again, but now with the maturity of one's life experience. Such a memory may have been slumbering deeply for decades in the unconscious, and now resurfaces to be assessed from the perspective of mature life experience. Such an occurrence is immensely fertile and stimulates a wealth of inner life forces.

What is the secret of remaining young in mind and soul? It is certainly not a nostalgic attitude of reminiscences about "the good old days of youth, when everything used to be so beautiful and not at all how life is now." It is the inner transformation of the experiences of our young days that keeps us young and makes us valuable to other human beings. This inner transformation represents the fruit of what was planted at one time into our souls when we were children. Impulses that are closely linked to human life and to our bodies are transformed in remarkable ways.

I would like to give just one example of such a transformation. There are people who, having reached a very old age, radiate a wholesome atmosphere on others in their company. They do not even need to speak words of wisdom; simply through their presence, they radiate a feeling of inner well-being on those around them so that their company is always welcome. They spread a kind of blessing. Where does this gift originate?

When we study, we consider only the years of childhood and schooling. In this way, education remains merely an external study. To study it in depth demands an extension of one's observations and interest over the entire span of life—from birth to death. And if we observe human life from the viewpoint of the kind of education I advocate, we find that this gift of blessing is rooted in an earlier natural veneration for one's educators, experienced during childhood. I would like to go even further and say that no one can spread arms and hands in inner admiration and reverence, in blessing, unless one has learned to fold hands in admiring or reverent prayer as a child. Over the course of human life, the inner experience of veneration is transformed into an ability to bless at a time of life when such blessing can affect others beneficially.

Once again, only when we include an entire lifetime in our observations can we practice a truly living education. In this case, one would not want to teach children rigid or fixed concepts. If we were to bind a child of five for a time in a tight-fitting garment that would not allow further growth—I am speaking hypothetically of course, for this does not happen— we would commit a dreadful and heinous crime in the child's physical life. But this is just what we do to the child's soul life when we teach definitions intended to remain unchanged, definitions that the child's memory is expected to carry, fixed and unaltered, throughout life. It is most important that we give the child only flexible ideas and concepts, capable of further growth—physical, soul, and spiritual growth. We must avoid teaching fixed concepts and instead bring concepts that change and grow with the child. We should never nurture an ambition to teach children something to be remembered for all of life, but should convey only mobile ideas. Those who are serious about learning the art of education will understand this.

You will not misunderstand when I say it is obvious that not every teacher can be a genius. But every teacher can find the situation where there are some boys and girls to be taught who, later in life, will show much greater intelligence than that of their current teachers. Real teachers should always be aware that some of the students sitting before them may one day far outshine them in intelligence and in other ways. True artists of education never assume that they are intellectually equal to the children sitting before them.

The basis of all education is the ability to use and bring to fulfillment whatever can be gained from the arts. If we derive writing and reading from painting, we are already applying an artistic approach. But we should be aware also of the immense benefits that can be derived from the musical element, especially for training the child's will. We can come to appreciate the role of the musical element only by basing education on real and true knowledge of the human being.

Music, however, leads us toward something else, toward eurythmy. Eurythmy is an art that we could say was developed from spiritual-scientific research according to the demands of our time. Out of a whole series of facts essential to knowledge of the human being, contemporary science knows only one little detail—that for right-handed people (that is, for the majority of people) the speech center is in the third left convolution of the brain, whereas for those who are left-handed it is on the right side of the brain. This is a mere detail. Spiritual science shows us further, which is fundamental to education, that all speech derives from the limb movements, broadly speaking, performed during early childhood.

Of course, the child's general constitution is important here, and this is much more significant than what results from more or less fortuitous external circumstances. For example, if a child were to injure a foot during the earlier years, such an injury does not need to have a noticeable influence in connection with what I now have in mind. If we inquire into the whole question of speech, however, we find that, when we appropriate certain impulses rooted in the limb system of speech, we begin with walking—that is, with every gesture of the legs and feet. Within the movements of the extremities—for instance in the feet—something goes through a mysterious inner, organic transformation into an impulse within the speech organs situated at the very front. This connection lives, primarily, in forming the consonants. Likewise, the way a child uses the hands is the origin of habitual speech forms. Speech is merely gestures that are transformed. When we know how speech is formed from consonants and vowels, we see the transformed limb movements in them. What we send into the world when we speak is a kind of "gesturing in the air."

An artistic pedagogical method makes it possible for us to bring what can flow from real knowledge of the human being into education. Through such a method, those who will educate in the sense of this pedagogical art are made into artists of education. There is nothing revolutionary at the basis of this education—just something that will stimulate new impulses, something that can be incorporated into every educational system—because it has sprung from the most intimate human potential for development.

Naturally, this necessitates various rearrangements of lessons and teaching in general, some of which are still very unusual. I will mention only one example: If one endeavors to practice the art of education according to the Waldorf methods, the natural goal is to work with the life of the child in concentrated form. This makes it impossible to teach arithmetic from eight to nine o'clock, for example, as is customary in many schools today, then history from nine to ten, and yet another subject from ten to eleven, and in this way, teaching all the subjects in haphazard sequence. In the Waldorf school, we have arranged the schedule so that for three to four weeks the same main lesson subject is taught every day from eight to ten in the morning; therefore the students can fully concentrate on and live in one main lesson subject. If what has thus been received is forgotten later, this does not offer a valid objection to our method, because we succeed by this method in nurturing the child's soul life in a very special way.

This was all meant merely as an example to show how a spiritual-scientific knowledge of the human being can lead to the development of an art of education that makes it possible again to reach the human being, not by an extraneous means, like those of experimental pedagogy or experimental psychology, but by means that allow the flow of life from our own inmost being into the child's inmost being.

When entering earthly life, human beings not only receive what is passed on by heredity through their fathers and mothers, but they also descend as spirit beings from the spiritual world into this earthly world. This fact can be applied practically in education when we have living insight into the human being. Basically, I cannot think of impressions more wonderful than those received while observing a young baby develop as we participate inwardly in such a gradual unfolding. After the infant has descended from the spiritual world into the earthly world, we can observe what was blurred and indistinct at first, gradually taking on form and shape. If we follow this process, we feel direct contact with the spiritual world, which is incarnating and unfolding before our very eyes, right here in the sensory world. Such an experience provides a sense of responsibility toward one's tasks as a teacher, and with the necessary care, the art of education attains the quality of a religious service. Then, amid all our practical tasks, we feel that the gods themselves have sent the human being into this earthly existence, and they have entrusted the child to us for education. With the incarnating child, the gods have given us enigmas that inspire the most beautiful divine service.

What thus flows into the art of education and must become its basis comes primarily from the teachers themselves. Whenever people air their views about educational matters, they often say that one shouldn't just train the child's intellect, but should also foster the religious element, and so on. There is much talk of that kind about what should be cultivated in children. Waldorf education speaks more about the qualities needed in the teachers; to us the question of education is principally a question of finding the right teachers.

When the child reaches puberty, the adolescent should feel: "Now, after my feeling and willing have been worked on at school, I am ready to train my thinking; now I am becoming mature enough to be dismissed into life." What meets us at this stage, therefore, is like a clear call coming from the students themselves when we learn to understand them. Anthroposophic knowledge of the human being is not meant to remain a theory for the mystically inclined or for idle minds. It wants to lead directly into life. Our knowledge of the human being is intended to be a practice, the aspect of real life closest to the human soul; it is connected most directly with our duty to the *becoming* human being. If we learn to educate in this way, in harmony with human nature, the following reassuring thought-picture will rise before us: We are carrying into the future something required by the future! Our cultural life has brought much suffering and complication to people everywhere; it is a reminder of the importance of our work in confronting the challenge of human evolution.

It is often said (ad nauseam, in fact) that the social question is really a question of cultural and spiritual life. Whenever we say that, it should make us aware that the roots of the difficulties in contemporary life are the inner obstacles, and that these must be overcome. Oh, how people today pass each other by without understanding! There is no love, no intimate interest in the potential of other human beings! Human love, not theories, can solve social problems. Above all, one thing is necessary to make possible the development of such an intimate and caring attitude, to effect again direct contact between one soul and another so that social ideas do not become merely theoretical demands: we must learn to harmonize social life in the right way by paying attention to the institution where teachers and children relate. The best seed to a solution of the social question is planted through the way social relationship develops between children and teachers at school. To educators, much in this art of education will feel like taking care of the seed, and through a realistic imagination of the future—it can never be utopian—what they have placed into the human beings entrusted to their care will one day blossom.

Just as we are meant to have before our eyes the entire course of human life when we educate children, with this same attitude we should view also the entire life of society, in its broadest aspects. To work as an educator means to work not for the present, but for the future! The child carries the future, and teachers will be carried, in the same way, by the most beautiful pedagogical attitude if they can remind themselves every moment of their lives: Those we have to educate were sent to us by higher beings. Our task is to lead our students into earthly life in a right and dignified way. Working in a living way with the children, helping them to find their way from the divine world order into the earthly world order—this must penetrate our art of education through and through, as an impulse of feeling and will, in order to meet the most important demands for human life today.

This is the goal of Waldorf pedagogy. What we have achieved in these few years may justify the conviction that a living knowledge of the human being arising from spiritual science can prove fertile for human existence in general and, through it, for the field of education, which is the most important branch of practical life.

10

Moral and Physical Education

THE HAGUE — NOVEMBER 19, 1923

The desire has been expressed that I should say more about Waldorf education. Because today's meeting had not been arranged yet when I spoke to you last Wednesday, tonight's talk may have to be somewhat aphoristic.

A few days ago I pointed out how the art of education as discussed here is meant to be based on true knowledge of the human being. Such a knowledge and insight regarding the human being must be comprehensive—that is, it must consider more than the physical and soul aspects of the human being and include the entire human being, made up of body, soul, and spirit working together as a unified whole.

On the other hand, I have also emphasized that, if we want to practice a real art of education, we must keep in mind the life-span of each student from birth to death, because much of what is implanted through education during the first life period, with regard to both health and illness, often manifests only during the last stages of a person's life. If teachers and educators consider only the students' present physical and soul-spiritual conditions, and if they develop their methods only according to what they see at that particular stage, they will not be capable of laying the proper foundations for a balanced and healthy development of their students in later years, thus enabling them to grow into strong, harmonious, and able people. To lay such a foundation, however, is precisely the aim of the art of education we are speaking of here. Because of this goal, our education is not in any way one-sided. One could easily believe that, because this education is the offspring of anthroposophical spiritual science, it would tend one-sidedly toward a spiritual perspective. But this is just not the case. Simply because it stays conscientiously focused on the entire human being, the physical aspect of its students receives the same full consideration that the soul-spiritual aspect receives. One could even say that the educational treatment of the child's soul and spirit is dealt with so that whatever the educator develops in the child will affect the physical organization in the best possible way.

In the Waldorf school in Stuttgart, as well as in other schools that follow similar educational principles and methods, we educate in order that the spiritual may have the best possible effect on the students' physical organization with every step toward a spiritual development. This is how it has to be in a true and genuine art of education. In children the soul and spiritual spheres are not yet distinct from the physical body as they are in adults.

We all know the difficulties that today's so-called philosophers encounter when trying to clearly picture the relationship between the spiritual and physical aspects of the human being. On the one side is the spiritual aspect. It is experienced inwardly through thinking and the soul life. Essentially, it is completely different from what we meet when studying the human physical body in physiology and anatomy. It is not easy to build a bridge from what we experience inwardly as our own soul and spirit to what an examination of the physical human body offers.

If one observes the child's development without prejudice, however, and if one has an eye for what is happening during the change of teeth, when the child undergoes its first important metamorphosis in life, one cannot help realizing that at this point the child's entire soul life goes through a great change. Previously, the child's representations emerged in an elemental, dreamy way. During this stage of life, we witness the development of memory; good observers will notice a transformation of the memory during, or because of, the change of teeth. Observation shows that until the change of teeth, the inner activity involved in remembering—that is, the inner activity that lives in memory—is really in the nature of a habit developed through the physical body. The child remembers—indeed, remembers remarkably well. This remembering, however, feels more like practiced repetition of an activity that has become an acquired skill. Indeed, memory as a whole during the first period of life really is an inner skill, the development of an inner habit. Only from the change of teeth onward, does a child start looking back on past experiences—that is, surveying past experiences in its mind—in a kind of review. In the evolving of memory, the soul life of the child undergoes a radical change.

The child's ability to form representations presents us with the same picture. When you look without bias at a young child's mental imagery, you will find that the will forces are very active. The child under seven cannot yet separate inner will experience from the experience of will in thinking. This separation begins during the change of teeth. In other words, with the change of teeth, the child's soul life goes through a complete metamorphosis. But what has actually happened? What is revealed as the child's true soul life after the change of teeth obviously couldn't have appeared from nothing. It must have been there already, but it did not manifest in the same way as during the later stage. It was active in the organic forces of growth and nourishment. It was an organic force that transformed into the force of memory, into freed soul forces.

If we want to progress in education in a way that is proper and professional, we must develop the same inner scientific courage shown in modern physics. There the concept of "latent heat" has been accepted, a concept that implies heat is bound to certain substances without radiating any externally measurable warmth. If, however, through some outer process this heat is drawn from the substance, it becomes so-called "liberated heat." Previously it had been "latent" heat. In physics we are used to such a concept. We should have the courage to form a similar concept when speaking about the human being. We should say: With the change of teeth the child's soul life has been liberated. Previously it was latent, bound to organic forces of growth, and worked in the form of nutrition and growth processes. Some of these forces, needed for later life, are still retained there, but part of them have separated off to become transformed into the liberated life of soul.

If these matters are not merely spoken of abstractly (and they need to be talked about), if as a teacher one can observe them concretely, a great wonder hidden in an intimate, tender, and refined way is revealed. The greatest wonder to be experienced in the world is for an attentive observer to watch the as yet indistinct features of an infant's face gradually assume more definition, and the jerky, undirected movements become more and more coordinated into meaningful limb movements. It is wonderful to see something rise to the surface of the whole organism from the child's center. If we can follow it with the open eyes of an artist, we experience wonderful world secrets in this unfolding of form and figure.

Similarly, when the child reaches school age—that is, during the change of teeth—we can see how what was working before through the forces of growth, is now liberated and develops as the child's life of soul. If we see this happening concretely and in detail, enthusiasm for education really awakens in us. It then becomes possible to gradually and appropriately guide the forces that had lived within the child until the second dentition.

Until the change of teeth, the child is a being of will—not in the same sense as a human being in later life, but a being of will who, at the same time, is completely a sense being. The following is meant as a metaphor but, if I may express myself in this way, the child really is one great and comprehensive sense organ. Within each sense organ, there lives more than the ability to perceive; there is also a certain will force, although in the actual sense organs this element of will is somewhat hidden. Likewise, in the will element of the child, the will lives like a sense organ until the coming of the second dentition. The child perceives everything in the surroundings in a much more intimate and sensitive way, and in such a way that everything is imitated inwardly, right down to the most internal organic formations. The child is a refined imitator. It is interesting that the child not only reacts to what is seen in the movements and gestures of other people (and of course the child also learns to speak by imitating what is heard), the child not only perceives these outer things, but also imitates people's moods, even their thoughts. One should be aware of life's imponderables. While in the proximity of a young child, we should not allow ourselves even one impure thought, because the fine processes of vibrations, set in motion by our thoughts, are imitated by the child's physical organism. Usually, people are totally unaware of such interplay between one human being and another. And scientific opinion is still fairly vague about this.

Permit me an aside to illustrate the strange relationships, not just between human beings, but even between a human being and an animal. It is something that does not easily fit into what one can perceive with one's eyes in the ordinary ways of sense perception, and it touches on the supersensible element to which I have frequently referred during the last few days. Some time ago, there was much talk about the "counting horses." I have not actually seen the main performing horses, which, as far as I know, were kept in Elberfeld, but I did observe one of these horses in action: It was the horse belonging to Mister von Osten in Berlin. I was able to study this horse and all its achievements. Spectators who observed superficially what was happening could see Mister von Osten standing next to his horse, presenting it with simple problems of arithmetic. The horse stamped the answers with one of its hooves, and this struck the onlookers as a great miracle.

However, ordinary members of the public were not the only ones to come and see this wonder; among the audience was also a university lecturer who wrote a treatise about Mister von Osten's horse. It is a very interesting book, although one might disagree with it. Now this university lecturer came to a very peculiar conclusion. He could not arrive at a proper explanation of the fact that Mister von Osten's horse could stamp "eleven" after being asked, "What is five plus six?" Because it is obvious to anyone who knows the limitations of such a creature that the horse could not possibly calculate numbers with anything like human sense. Consequently, it would be nonsense for anyone to believe the horse really could answer simple arithmetic problems.

To discover how these results were obtained, one needs to ponder what was happening below the surface. Still, the fact remained: the horse did answer the questions correctly. This led the university lecturer to theorize that Mister von Osten continued to count numbers up to eleven silently in his mind as he was asking the question, "Five plus six is?" And when he reached the number representing the answer, he made a very subtle facial expression. The author of the treatise believed that the subtle play in Mister von Osten's face was giving the horse the hint, and while he counted to eleven, specific vibrations emanated from him that were different from those accompanying previous numbers. According to the lecturer, the horse was supposed to notice these vibrations, which caused it to stamp the answer with one of its hooves. Thus, the trick was presumably due to the fine vibrations the horse was able to perceive.

So much for the lecturer's theory. There is, however, one flaw, and the lecturer was well aware of it. Apart from the horse, any observer should be able to detect the fine play of expressions in Mister von Osten's face. The author of the treatise explained this away by saying that human beings cannot detect such a play of features—which amounts to an admission that a horse had a greater capacity for observing a human face than a university lecturer! This really goes a little too far, and the crux of the matter is actually very different.

While I was studying the relationship between Mister von Osten and his horse, the most important factor for me was the strange feeling rapport with the horse, which Herr von Osten kept going all the time by taking sugar lumps from his pocket and giving them to his horse while it was answering the problems. In this way an animalistic feeling of sympathy arose. Here, I was witnessing one of life's imponderables. This feeling of gratitude must have enabled the horse to perceive what was in its master's mind, not through the play of features on Mister von Osten's face, but on the waves of the animals's own feelings of gratitude for the sugar lumps, enabling it to know to stamp when hearing its master call out the number eleven as answer to the question, "What is six plus five?" The secret of this phenomenon was an intimate relationship between master and horse, enabling the horse to feel its way into what lived in von

Osten's mind. This is how a kind of telepathy of sentiments came about. I do not wish to go into this matter further, but only wanted to mention it in this context. I came to my conclusion after careful consideration. I mention it as proof that even in more primitive creatures, empathy can occur between one living being and another.

A similar thing happens very much in the young child. The child also experiences in other people what cannot be seen with the eyes or heard with the ears, and these experiences have a lasting inner effect. Consequently we should not allow a single unworthy thought to enter our minds while around a young child, even though we cannot possibly prove the existence of such a thought by specific vibrations. Yes, the child is a very fine sense organ and completely an imitator. You must try to realize what this means. You must imagine that whatever happens in the proximity of the child will have an effect right into the physical organization, even if the effect cannot be proved with the aid of crude external instruments. If, for example, a choleric father bursts into tempers in the presence of a child, and if such outbursts become part of daily life, the child will experience these scenes right into its blood circulation and into the formation of its glandular secretions.

The whole physical organization of the child will be formed according to what the soul and spirit experienced from the surroundings. The child is an imitator during the first period of life, up to the second dentition. But this form of imitation has a direct effect on its physical organism. In the blood, in the blood vessels, and in the fine structure of the nervous system, we all carry throughout our lives a certain constitution resulting from what influenced us during the first life period. From this point of view, the very first education or upbringing, either in the parental home or anywhere else in the child's environment, very naturally amounts to a physical education par excellence. All spiritual influences around the child also enter the physical, bodily realm of the child. Whatever the delicate organization of the child absorbs in the bodily realm has lasting effects during its entire earthly life until the moment of death.

When a child has gone through the second dentition, this fine sense perception decreases. The child's own ideation begins to separate from sense perceptions. But the essential quality of the sense perceptions, which during the first life period completely sets the tone, is the pictorial element, because the child naturally cannot yet comprehend abstract concepts. Introducing these to a child would be an act of gross folly. Living in pictures is of paramount importance for the child's life of ideation—indeed, for the child's entire soul life until the beginning of puberty—and any intellectual teaching before the age of puberty is a sin against the development of the child's entire soul life. A child needs to be taught through a pictorial and artistic presentation. During this stage the relationship between teacher and student is immensely important. I would like to clarify this with an example.

To anyone who wants to introduce a higher truth to the child—for example, the truth of the immortality of the human soul—it will be obvious that one has to begin in the form of an image. One could gradually lead the child to the concept of immortality by saying, "Look at the caterpillar that turns into a cocoon." One can show the child a cocoon, or a chrysalis. Then one shows how a butterfly emerges. Finally one can tell the child that the human soul is resting in the body, just as the butterfly rests in the chrysalis, except that the human soul is not outwardly visible; nevertheless, it flies out of the body after death.

Of course, such an approach is not meant to demonstrate the immortality of the soul. This approach would provoke legitimate objections that have already been voiced by various people. All I have in mind is to show how one can give the child a picture of the immortality of the human soul. The child will become acquainted with the proofs at a later stage in life. The point is that between the change of teeth and puberty the child must receive content in the form of images. Such pictures enliven the soul and make it fertile for the entire life to come.

In this context there are two ways to proceed. Some teachers may feel vastly superior in intelligence to the child, whom they consider immature and as yet ignorant. This is a very natural feeling, or so it would appear, at least—how else could a teacher teach a child? Consequently, such teachers may think up a picture of the emerging butterfly for the benefit of the ignorant child and then describe it. They will not be very successful, for their efforts will make little impact upon the child's soul.

There is, however, another possibility; a teacher may not feel at all intelligent, and that the child is stupid. By the way, I am not suggesting here that teachers should assume the opposite either. Nevertheless, one can take a different approach. A teacher may hold the view that this picture reveals a truth that spiritual powers have revealed in a natural process, and in this case one believes in the truth of this picture. One really believes in the truth of this simile. A teacher may well feel and believe that the creative forces of nature have placed before our eyes a picture of what actually happens on a higher level when a human soul leaves the physical body at death. If one permeates such a picture with one's own belief, thus feeling fully united with it, and if one speaks to a child with the naturally ensuing enthusiasm, then such a picture will live in the child and become fertile for life.

This example shows that being smart in itself is not necessarily the hallmark of a good teacher. Of course intelligence and cleverness will help in many ways and, in any case, it is obviously preferable and better if the teacher is clever rather than foolish. Still, cleverness alone does not make a teacher into a real artist of education. Artistry in teaching is achieved only when the teacher faces the world with a mind and soul that brings about a truly living relationship between teacher and student, so that what lives in the teacher can continue in the soul of the child. Then a natural sense of authority will develop in the child rather than one artificially imposed.

All teaching during the time between the change of teeth and puberty has to be built on this natural sense of authority. This is why we must place the greatest emphasis on the use of a pictorial approach during the early school years (from around six to approximately fourteen). During these years we must introduce our subject matter in images. At the latest possible time (maybe not until the approach of puberty between thirteen and fourteen) we can gradually introduce subjects that need to be understood abstractly. It is best to wait as long as possible before drawing children out of a direct, realistic experience of life in their surroundings. This is because, even between the change of teeth and puberty, something is left, although weakened, that was present during the first tender age of childhood up to the second dentition; even now, everything a child encounters from the outside world has aftereffects within the physical corporeality.

During the second life period, whatever the child perceives now has a less powerful effect on the organic constitution than during the years preceding the change of teeth. Nevertheless, how teaching content is introduced to children matters very much in how it effects physical development. Here the teacher must achieve something that cannot be accomplished theoretically, but only through the artistic approach that must weave and work throughout education. Let us again keep to a single detail; no matter how much one insists that a child's memory should not be overloaded—a request that, in the abstract, is correct—it is nevertheless in the child's nature to develop memory. The child's memory forces need to be cultivated. But it is essential that, through proper knowledge of the growing child, the teacher should be able to feel and observe how much pressure upon the memory becomes harmful. A very great deal depends on this faculty of good judgment.

Teachers who have become artists of education will see in the students' outer appearance something like a barometer, which will tell them how much memorizing they may expect from the students and when to stop appealing to the powers of memory. Here are the facts: What happens when we strain the students' memory too much? Where does the force of memory originate? Remember what happens during the second dentition— that the forces of growth working in the nutritive processes are liberated and now work in the realm of the soul. This also happens continually, though to a lesser extent, later in life, which is why we need forces of growth through the digestive processes of nutrition. The entire human life is a transformation of healthy forces of growth, working to build the organs and the blood, into liberated soul forces.

What happens in the child at the change of teeth—in a big way and all at once, as it were—happens again and again, whenever we absorb something into memory. Whatever works on us when we perceive something with the senses, or when we perceive something in words, affects our entire physical organism. Anyone expected to remember something—by memorizing a poem, for example—will experience the necessity for the physical organism's cooperation. Just look at someone who is told to remember something; you will observe much physical activity in the act of memorizing. What has found a seat in the physical organism cannot be remembered yet, however, because it is linked to the forces of growth and nourishment, and it must first be transformed into soul forces. In the realm of the soul, this is done through memory.

Whenever I give a child too much to remember, I use up too much of the child's life forces, the vital forces; consequently, if I can see through the entire process, I will notice the child becoming pale and anxious, because I am appropriating organic forces. One needs to watch for this pallor and for subsequent anxiety and nervousness. You see, by aiming continuously and rigorously at training the child's memory, we weaken the growth forces. If we activate the students' memory too much, we stunt their physical growth. Such retarding of the forces of growth is caused by an exaggerated appeal to the memory forces. What is done to the students' organism in such a case is expressed years later in various metabolic illnesses caused by harmful deposits of uric acid or kindred substances.

The most important point is this: We must guide children's education in ways that work in proper harmony with their physical organism. We must avoid planting seeds of metabolic diseases for later life. Too little is known about the links between old-age gout and rheumatism, and the wrong kind of schooling through overtaxing students' memory; if more were known, we would stand on a more realistic ground in education. One would then also recognize the fallacy of separating education into academic and physical subjects, since everything one does in the academic subjects works into the physical constitution of the child, and, conversely, everything one does in physical education works back again into the child's spiritual conditions. If you perceive a melancholic temperament in one child, or a sanguine temperament in another, this observation should immediately color your treatment of the two different types of children.

If you notice, for example, that a child's pronounced melancholic character is endangering the physical health, then the parents must be contacted. The Waldorf school is built entirely on direct and close contact with the parents. In the Waldorf school, the students' parents are called to parent meetings every month, and sometimes even more frequently. Matters that require cooperation between home and school are discussed in such meetings. Many points must be brought to the parents' notice. For example, there may be a child of a strongly melancholic temperament. One recognizes that this disposition is connected with the secretion of the liver, and that this in turn is related to the sugar consumption. In meetings with the parents, every possibility is offered to reach an agreement to increase the sugar intake by sweetening the child's foods. As an educator, one always has to consider the physical aspect, insofar as it has a spiritual counterpart. On the other hand, one educates the child so that, with the help of the spiritual, one can effect the best possible conditions for physical health.

Let us now take the opposite case, not an overloading of memory, but the opposite. I am thinking of modern teachers who may advocate never straining the students' memory, and who consequently omit altogether the cultivation and training of the memory in their teaching. I often feel tempted to say to those who always clamor for the observational methods of object lessons: If one neglects the training of the memory, one will also notice physical symptoms in the children. The child's skin becomes unhealthily red. The child begins to complain about all kinds of inner pressures, and finally one realizes that the child is growing at an alarming rate.

By following such a case, we may notice that the neglect of memory training is weakening the physical body's ability to absorb food into various organs. If memory is insufficiently stimulated, the stomach reacts by not secreting enough acids, or the acids secreted are not adequate for a proper digestion. This tendency will spread over the whole organism, and the ability to absorb necessary substances decreases. After many years, one may discover that the physical body of such a person is always hungry, yet it cannot function properly, organically speaking. Such a person has a tendency toward lung diseases and kindred illnesses. Any education based on real knowledge of the human being will not drift into a "never-never land" of vague spirituality, but will continually observe the whole human being, encompassing spirit, soul, and body. This is absolutely essential to the art of education.

Teaching must be arranged so that there is enough variety within the lessons. On the one hand, students must be kept occupied intellectually. (The intellectual approach is used only for subjects directed to the immediate realm of the soul; the intellectual element as such must be avoided until the approach of puberty.) In physical training, the children are kept busy with gymnastics, eurythmy, and similar activities. If the children's day is organized on the basis of abstract requirements, however (and this happens only too often for mere scheduling convenience), one's efforts are unlikely to be fruitful. One must keep in mind that, when we teach children reading, writing, and arithmetic, which work most of all on their soul life, there is an opposite process going on at the same time in the physical organism, indicating that everything engaging the child's head has the opposite effect in the limb and motor system. It is incorrect to say, for example, that children tire less in gymnastics lessons than in reading or writing lessons, which is what experimental psychology claims to have determined. In reality, if you put gymnastics between two other lessons—for example, an arithmetic lesson from nine to ten A.M., gymnastics from ten to eleven, and history from eleven to twelve—then the child, having had gymnastics in the previous lesson, is not rested for the history lesson, but quite the contrary.

The real point is something very different. A person who can apply real knowledge of the human being knows that something is always working in the physical organism, even if only subconsciously. Within the child, much remains only partially conscious. It escapes observation, therefore, and is not taken up consciously later. It then happens that, through the activity of soul and spirit, a process of desire is stimulated. This must be allowed to proceed so that our teaching does not remain external to the child. Lessons that appeal to soul and spirit must be arranged so that, through the lessons, an inner physical mood for gymnastics is stimulated. If I engage a child in gymnastics who has no inner organic desire for this activity, the child will soon show signs of being unable to direct the forces inward as a continuation of outer movements. Everything that is developed while the body is engaged in physical movements must be prolonged inwardly. While the body is moving, inner metabolic processes occur. Something we could call a process of combustion, transformed into conditions for life, occurs. And what is thus activated, continues to work throughout the organism.

If I allow a child to do gymnastics when there is no inner desire for it, the child cannot cope with these inner metabolic processes. As a result, I may notice the child becoming somewhat emotional through doing gymnastics in these circumstances. All kinds of passionate feelings may develop. If I force a child to do gymnastics, a child who has no organic desire for it, I can arouse an unhealthy inner mood that can even lead to fits of anger. Such a mood may become a chronic part of a child's characterological disposition.

All this can be avoided. The enhancement of a healthy physical development can be achieved only when, as an artist of education, one is guided by the right instincts of soul to give gymnastics lessons their proper place in the timetable relative to other subjects, where soul and spirit are engaged so that a desire for gymnastics is awakened. Then the organism can use properly the forces developed through the activity of gymnastics.

It is very important that the teacher be a kind of artist, who can affect the child with an artistic outlook, but also with a tremendous sense of responsibility. While the latter is not absolutely imperative in other artistic pursuits—where the material used is not living—it is essential for teaching. The teacher works with the growing human being—that is, with this wonderful interplay of thousands of forces working into each other. This interplay cannot be comprehended through a theoretical kind of pedagogy any more than one could teach someone to regulate the digestion through theoretical physiology. It can be comprehended only through intuition.

Consequently, anyone who educates out of full knowledge of human nature will train their students' spiritual faculties in a way that enhances the healthy development of their physical bodies. They will arrange the physical aspect of education so it can be the basis for an all-around development of the spiritual aspect. This development, however, is only possible with the kind of intimate adjustment between teacher and student that I have indicated with the example of the emerging butterfly as a picture of the human soul's immortality. If such a close-knit relationship exists, the natural feeling for the authority of the teacher, which I presented as an essential feature in education, will develop naturally. To the students the teacher becomes the unquestioned representative of truth, beauty, and goodness. The child should not have to judge abstractly what is true or false, beautiful or ugly, good or evil; this faculty of moral judgments belongs to a later age. The student's sense of truth should be guided by the teacher's revered personality. The teacher has to be the portal for the experience of beauty, truth, and goodness. The student's sense of truth will be the natural consequence of the right relationship between teacher and child.

Something absolutely essential is achieved in this way for the moral development of the child, and it has to be accomplished by the proper means. For, from the moral perspective, a young person is morally crippled by a premature introduction of moral commandments in the form of "Thou shalt" and "Thou shalt not." Children need to experience what is good or evil through the living medium of a teacher. For this to happen, the teacher's attitude must engender in children a spontaneous love for good, a pleasure in what is good, and a feeling of aversion toward evil. In our moral teaching, we must not insist on moral commandments, or the prohibition of what we consider morally wrong; please note this carefully, Ladies and Gentlemen, because much depends on precisely this nuance. We must nurture in children, between the change of teeth and puberty, an experience of what is good or evil in the emotional sphere— not in will impulses. The good must bring inner pleasure. We must engender love and sympathy for the good before we turn it into a moral duty by appealing to the will sphere. What eventually must become moral action first has to grow from an experience of moral pleasure or aversion in the realm of feeling.

Again, we work best toward this goal when we approach it through imagery. If teachers have the necessary imagination to present to their students the moral or immoral actions of well-known historical people, which the children will then wish either to emulate or to shun, if teachers know how to describe a historical situation in such a lively way that they evoke inner pleasure or displeasure in the students, or if they invent such stories (which is even better because through their own creativity they are more closely linked to this inner pleasure or displeasure in students), then moral appreciation is awakened in the students' feeling life.

And then something interesting will happen; when the children reach sexual maturity, the right moral impulses for the will life will develop out of a properly conducted feeling of moral pleasure or displeasure, just as sexual love grows naturally from physical development. The hallmark of a right education is that whatever is meant to develop through inner maturity of soul out of a previous budding stage, will do so on its own. This approach is far better than grafting preconceived moral codes onto students. If we wish to cultivate morality, it must grow in the sphere of the will. This growth will occur only when we plant the seeds for it in young children. We can do this by kindling feelings of pleasure for good and feelings of aversion for evil during the stage of life when children need to experience love and sympathy for the educator.

Everything depends on bringing the appropriate content to children at the right time of life. That content will then work itself out properly in later life. Just as when we plant an acorn in the soil, branches, leaves, and fruits will grow above it, so when we plant the right seeds within children at seven or eight in the form of moral pleasure or displeasure, the appropriate sense of moral duty will evolve as the child turns seventeen or eighteen.

It is especially important in this sense to know how to guide the child's religious development. It cannot be genuine and inwardly true if it is brought about solely through religious stories or creeds; it depends rather on the teacher's ability to engender a religious mood in the child. Religious education achieves its goals only when the religious mood rises spontaneously from the depths of children's souls. However, if the teachers themselves are not permeated with a religious mood, it cannot develop in the child. If, on the other hand, this mood is there in the teachers, they need only do as we do in our so-called free religion lessons in the Waldorf school.

I want to emphasize strongly at this point that the Waldorf school is definitely not an ideological school. We do not wish to educate students to become young anthroposophists; but we do wish to use our anthroposophical knowledge so that the school can become an organization using proper methods in the truest sense. With the help of anthroposophy, we want to develop the right methods of education in every sphere. It is simply untrue to say that the Waldorf school's intention is to indoctrinate students into anthroposophy. To prevent such an unfounded rumor from gaining ground, I have given instructions for religion lessons to be given by members of the various religious denominations. This means that Roman Catholic children will receive their religious instruction from Roman Catholic priests, Protestant children from Protestant ministers, and so on.

Due to the inherent circumstances of the Waldorf school's beginning, however, many of our first students were children of religious dissenters. For these children, "free" Christian religious lessons—that is, *free* of established denominations—were initially included on a trial basis in the Waldorf school schedule. We were gratified to find that children of thoroughly atheistic parents attended these lessons with their parents' consent. One can truly say that these free religious lessons are supported extremely well. Nevertheless, we take great care not to be mistaken as a denominational or an ideological school, but to show that our interest is in the practice of definite educational methods.

One of these methods, for example, consists of introducing the appropriate lesson material in the right way and at the appropriate age. These free religious lessons are there only for children who attend them voluntarily. Admittedly these now include considerably more students than are receiving religious instruction from Catholic or Protestant religion teachers. We cannot be held responsible for this situation. Students feel greatly stimulated by these free religious lessons, which bear a thoroughly Christian viewpoint and character; otherwise students would shun them. I mention this merely as a fact and not with the intention of judging.

The religious lessons are based on the premise that a religious atmosphere can be created in every lesson and subject. Such an atmosphere is created in our school. When teachers, through their own soul mood, connect everything that exists in the sensory world to the supersensible and divine, everything they bring to their classes will naturally transcend the physical, not in a sentimental or vaguely mystical way, but simply as a matter of course. All that is needed for this is the necessary feeling of tact. Then everything introduced to the students in various subjects can be summed up, as it were, in a religious mood. Our few specific religion lessons are given as additional lessons during each week. What lives in all of the other lessons anyway, and leads students to the divine-spiritual, is brought together in the free religious lessons, and lifted to the divine and spiritual level, through interpretation of natural phenomena and observation of historical events. Eventually, through the right cultivation of the religious mood, the children will experience moral impulses as the divine speaking in human nature and in the human being.

To bring about the right cultivation of a religious mood, something easily overlooked nowadays needs to be developed in the children; an honest, entirely open, feeling of gratitude must be nurtured beginning at an early age. Certainly, love must grow in the natural relationship between teacher and student during the years between the change of teeth and puberty, and much care must be given in nurturing this love. Gratitude has to be developed so that children experience it for everything received. Whatever it may be, whatever has been received from another person calls forth a feeling of gratitude. An immense enrichment of the soul is achieved through the experience of this feeling of gratitude. One should see to it that, even in a very young child, a feeling of thankfulness is developed. If one does this, a feeling of gratitude will be transformed into love when the child enters the second period of life. In every situation in life, love will be colored through, permeated with gratitude. Even a superficial observation of social life demonstrates that a valuable impulse for the social question can be fostered when we educate people toward a greater feeling of gratitude for what their fellow human beings are doing. For this feeling of gratitude is a bridge from one human soul and heart to another; without gratitude, this bridge could never be built.

If people had a greater sense of gratitude toward other human beings, we would not see so much of what passes for social demands, social radicalism, and so on, occasionally of a rather grotesque kind. When I say this, I am not siding with one or another social group. My own contribution to the subject can be read in my book *Towards Social Renewal.*[1] However, if this feeling of gratitude is nurtured in the child at an early age, and experienced in the child's love for the teacher between the second dentition and puberty; if gratitude is encouraged to enter the child's soul so that with the arrival of sexual maturity the soul can unfold genuine love for other human beings, as well as for all of nature and the divine and spiritual beings; if gratitude becomes all-pervasive, then out of gratitude, the religious mood will develop in the human being. Gratitude toward the divine and spiritual powers sustaining life can be a tremendous protection for the soul. It is an important factor in the generation of inner warmth and a sense of security in life. The feeling of gratitude toward the divine and spiritual powers is in itself a great source of revitalization for our earthly life. I

---

1. *Towards Social Renewal: Basic Issues of the Social Question*, Rudolf Steiner Press, London, 1992. (Originally translated as *The Threefold Commonwealth*.)

would like to put it this way: *What intensifies the physical organic forces in the blood is comparable to what vitalizes the human soul spiritually when it develops love and gratitude toward the entire universe.*

Working in the art of education as we advocate avoids one-sidedly physical or spiritual-mental education. It allows instead the beneficial confluence of spirit working in matter and matter as the bearer of creative spirit. Then we educate the spiritual and the physical sides simultaneously. This is the only adequate way, because the human being is a unity of spirit and the physical. However, such an education must never degenerate into one-sided theorizing, but must remain a true art, an art that lives in the person of the teacher. But one needs to have faith that nature herself is the great artist working in harmony with divine, spiritual forces. Basically, unless one can lead abstract natural laws into an artistic appreciation, one does not understand what is weaving and living in nature.

What is the central point of such an attitude toward education? Today there is much talk about how children should be educated. Prescriptions are handed out for a more or less intellectual kind of education, or for more emphasis on the will aspect in education. Great! One talks a lot about children, and rightly so. Of course, children should be at the center of all educational endeavor. But this is possible only if each individual teacher is really capable of deep insight, with an artistic eye that can see the human being as an entity. That is why all realistic discussions about education ultimately come down to the question of finding the right teachers.

To do this, Waldorf pedagogy has been created from the work of the teachers' faculty meetings and various staff meetings. Ultimately, the faculty of teachers is the soul of the school, but this can be only when the various teachers can work together.

To conclude, let me say this: If one enters a school run according to the aims of this art of education, if one views the attitude of the teaching staff, from which everything radiates that happens in each class and affects each child, one would be reminded of the words above the door of the room where the teachers meet for their consultations, the ever admonishing words: "All your educational endeavors should bring out in you the urge for self-education! Your self-education is the seed for everything you do for your children. Indeed, whatever you achieve can only be a product and result of your self-education."

This must not remain just a more or less external admonishment; it must be engraved deeply into the heart, mind, and soul of every teacher. Ultimately, human beings are educated into becoming good citizens of the world, of use to their fellow human beings. Only one thing can and must be achieved in education, especially at a time when life has become so complex and demands so much constructive energy to supplant the forces of decay; this one thing is the recognition that true education, education toward love, will be fostered through the dedicated efforts of the head, the soul, and the heart of each individual teacher.

11

Educational Issues

LONDON — AUGUST 29, 1924

PART ONE

First of all I would like to express my heartfelt thanks to Mrs. Mackenzie for her kind words of greeting, and to all of you who have made the effort to meet again, at Professor Mackenzie's invitation, to discuss questions of education.

In the short time available little can be said about the educational methods based on anthroposophy, for their essence is in an educational practice that does not have fixed programs, nor clearly defined general concepts to encompass it. The main intention of Waldorf education is that its teachers should be able to look deeply into the nature of the child from a true and genuine knowledge of the human being, and that in the individuality of each child who has come down into the earthly realm, they should be able to experience a wondrous enigma, which the educator and the world can never hope to understand completely.

The teacher's practical task is to discern ways to approach the mystery, the enigma, that divine guiding spirits present us with each child who joins our contemporary society. The teacher's task begins at the age when the child discards the baby teeth, around the seventh year, and extends until the eighteenth or nineteenth year when, as a young man or woman, the student either goes out into life or enters higher education.

A few years ago, due to the devastating war, many new ideals, and certainly many illusions as well, emerged in Germany. At that time, the industrialist Emil Molt saw an opportunity to do something important for the workers in his factory. He felt that, by opening a school for their children, he could to some extent help reconcile his workers with their destiny as factory workers, and above all do something about what was then the great social demand of the time—he wanted to begin a school for his employees' children, where the children, although laborers' children, would get the best possible education imaginable.

This should make it clear immediately that the education I am representing here was not hatched from some ideas or from any plan for reform; it was, instead, born as a direct answer to a practical life situation. Emil Molt simply declared, "My workers have a total of a hundred and fifty children, and these children must be educated in the best way possible." This could happen within the anthroposophical movement because, as strange as it may sound to you, anthroposophists are neither theorists nor visionary dreamers, but practical people who take the pragmatic side of life seriously; indeed, we like to believe that practical matters are nurtured especially within the anthroposophical movement. In other words, the idea regarding this education was the direct result of a practical need.

In Stuttgart, where all this happened, the necessary conditions for starting such a school were soon created. At that time, a democratic legislation of schools did not yet exist; that came into force only with the subsequent democratically constituted assembly. We came just in time to begin the school before the emergence of a "free" school legislation, which forced a general levelling of all schools in Germany—paying lip service to freedom by enforcing fixed laws. So we were only just in time to open such a school. I must quickly add that the school authorities have always shown great understanding and cooperation ever since the school was founded. It was fortunately possible to begin "The Free Waldorf school" in complete freedom. Its name arose because of its association with the Waldorf-Astoria Factory.

I do not wish to imply in any way that state-trained teachers are inferior, and certainly not that they are poor teachers simply because they have passed a state exam! Nevertheless, I was granted freedom in my choice of teachers, regardless of whether they were state trained or not. It was left to my discretion whether my candidates would make good and efficient teachers, and it happens that most of the teachers at the Waldorf school, based on the educational principles I wish to speak about, are in fact not state trained.

However, the situation did not remain as it was then. The school was begun with a hundred and fifty students. In no time at all, anthroposophists living in Stuttgart also wanted to send their children to this school because the education it offered was supposed to be very good. Since then (only a few years ago) the school has grown to more than eight hundred children. Several grades, like our fifth and sixth grades, have three parallel classes.

A further step, perhaps not quite as practical (I don't want to judge this) was that Emil Molt, after deciding to open the school, asked me to provide the school with spiritual guidance and methods. It was only possible to give this guidance based on the spiritual research and knowledge of the human being that I represent. Our fundamental goal is to know the complete human being as a being of body, soul, and spirit, as a person grows from childhood, and to be able to read in the soul of the child what needs to be done each week, month, and year. Consequently, one could say our education is a teaching based entirely on knowledge of the child, and this knowledge guides us in finding the appropriate methods and principles.

I can give only general and sketchy outlines here of what is meant by knowledge of the human being. There is much talk nowadays about physical education, about the importance of not sacrificing physical education to the education of the child's mind and soul. However, to separate the physical aspect from that of the soul and spirit is in itself a great illusion, because in a young child, spirit, soul, and body form a unity. It is impossible to separate one realm from the other in early childhood.

To give an example, let us imagine a child at school; a child becomes more and more pale. The paling of the child is a physical symptom that the teacher should notice. If an adult becomes increasingly pale, one seeks the advice of a doctor, who will think of an appropriate therapy according to an understanding of the case. Teachers of an abnormally pale child must ask themselves whether this child was already that pale when entering the class, or if the child's complexion changed afterward. Lo and behold, they may realize that they themselves were the cause of the child's pallor, because of excessive demands on the child's memory forces. Consequently they will realize that they must reduce the pressure in this respect. Here is a case where physical symptoms reveal problems in the sphere of the soul. The child becomes pale because the memory has been overtaxed.

Then again, teachers may be faced with a different type of child; this time the child does not turn pale; on the contrary, the complexion becomes increasingly ruddy. This child appears to lack good will, gets restless, and turns into what is usually called a "hyperactive" child. The child lacks discipline, jumps up and down and cannot sit still for a moment, constantly wanting to run in and out. It is now up to the teacher to find the cause of these changes, and, lo and behold, it may be found (not always, because individual cases vary greatly and have to be diagnosed individually) that the child had been given too little to remember. This can easily happen because the appropriate amount of material to be remembered varies greatly from child to child.

As it happens, government inspectors visit our school. The authorities make sure that they know what is happening in our school! At the time when socialism was flourishing, one local director of education came to inspect the school, and I took him around to the various classes for three days. I pointed out that our physical education was intended to develop the students' spiritual capacities, and that we educate their mental-spiritual capacities in such a way that their physical bodies benefit, because the two form a unity. Thereupon the inspector exclaimed, "But in this case your teachers would have to know medicine as well, and that is not possible!" To which I answered, "I do not think so, but if it were indeed necessary, it would have to be done, because a teacher's training must ensure that the teacher is capable of thorough insight into the physical and spiritual background of the growing child."

Furthermore, if one has a child of the type just described, a child who becomes increasingly restless and who does not pale but, on the contrary, becomes flushed, one can think of all kinds of things to do. However, to help such a child, one has to make sure of the right treatment. And the right treatment may be very difficult to find, for insight into human nature must not limit its considerations to a certain period of time, such as from age seven to age fourteen, which is the time when the class teacher is with the children. One must realize that much of what happens during these seven years has consequences that manifest only much later. One might choose the comfortable ways of experimental psychology, which only considers the child's present state of development to decide what to do, but if one endeavors to survey the child's whole life from birth to death, one knows: When I give the child too little content to remember, I induce a tendency toward serious illness, which may not appear before the forty-fifth year; I may cause a layer of fat to form above the heart. One has to know what form of illness may be induced eventually through the education of the child's soul and spirit. Knowledge of the human being is not confined to an experiment with a student in the present condition, but includes knowledge of the whole human being—body, soul, and spirit—as well as a knowledge of what happens during various ages and stages of life.

When these matters become the basis for teaching, one will also find them relevant in the moral sphere. You may agree with me when I say that there are some people who, in ripe old age, give off an atmosphere of blessing to those in their company. They needn't say much, but nevertheless radiate beneficial influence to others merely by the expression in their eyes, their mere presence, arm gestures—saying little perhaps, but speaking with a certain intonation and emphasis, or a characteristic tempo. They can permeate whatever they say or do with love, and this is what creates the effect of blessing on those around them. What kind of people are they?

In order to explain this phenomenon with real insight into human life, one must look back to their childhood. One then finds that such people learned, in their childhood, to revere and pray to the spiritual world in the right way, for no one has the gift of blessing in old age who has not learned to fold his or her hands in prayer between the ages of seven and fourteen. This folding of the hands in prayer during the age of primary education enters deeply into the inner organization of the human being and is transformed into the capacity for blessing in old age. This example shows how different life stages are interrelated and interwoven in human life. When educating children, one educates for all of life—that is, during a person's younger years one may cultivate possibilities for moral development in old age.

This education does not encroach on human freedom. Human freedom is attacked primarily when a certain inner resistance struggles against a free will impulse. What I have been talking about is connected with freeing a person from inner impediments and hindrances.

This should suffice as an introduction to tonight's theme. When one tries to achieve a more intimate knowledge of human nature, observing it not just externally but also with the inner gaze directed more toward the spiritual, one discovers that human beings pass through clearly defined life periods.

The first three periods of life are of particular importance and interest for education. The first one has a more homogeneous character and lasts from birth to age seven—that is, until the time of the change of teeth. The second period of life extends from the change of teeth to puberty, around age fourteen. The third begins at puberty and ends in the twenties. It is easy to notice external physical changes, but only a trained capacity for observation will reveal the more hidden aspects of these different life periods.

Such observation shows that during the first seven years, roughly from birth to the change of teeth, the child's spirit, soul, and body are completely merged into a unity. Observe a child entering into this world, with open features still undifferentiated, movements uncoordinated, and without the ability to show even the most primitive human expressions, such as laughing or weeping. (A baby can cry, of course, but this crying is not really weeping; it does not spring from emotions of the soul because the soul realm has not yet developed independently.) All of this makes the child into a unique being, and indeed, the greatest wonder of the world. We observe a baby weekly and monthly; from an undefined physiognomy, something gradually evolves in the physical configuration of the little body, as if coming from a center. Soul qualities begin to animate not only the child's looks, but also the hand and arm movements. And it is a wonderful moment when, after moving about on hands and knees, the child first assumes the vertical posture. To anyone who can observe this moment, it appears as a most wonderful phenomenon.

When we perceive all this with spiritual awareness, which can be done, it shows us the following: There, in this unskillful little body, spirit is living, spirit that cannot yet control limb movements. This is still done very clumsily, but it is the same human spirit that, later on, may develop into a genius. It is there, hidden in the movements of arms and legs, in questing facial expression, and in the searching sense of taste.

Then we find that, from birth until the second dentition, the young child is almost entirely one sense organ. What is the nature of a sense organ? It surrenders fully to the world. Consider the eye. The entire visible world is mirrored in the eye and is contained in it. The eye is totally surrendered to the world. Likewise the child, though in a different way, is surrendered fully to the environment. We adults may taste sweet, bitter, or acid tastes on the tongue and with the palate, but the tastes do not penetrate our entire organism. Although we are not usually aware of it, it is nevertheless true to say that when the baby drinks milk the taste of the milk is allowed to permeate the entire organism. The baby lives completely like an eye, like one large sense organ. The differentiation between outer and inner senses occurs only later. And the characteristic feature is that, when a child perceives something, it is done in a state of dreamy consciousness.

If, for example, a very choleric father, a man who in behaviors, gestures, and attitudes is always ready to lose his temper, and displays the typical symptoms of his temperament around a child, then the child, in a dreaming consciousness, perceives not only the outer symptoms, but also the father's violent temperament. The child does not recognize temperamental outbursts as such, but perceives the underlying disposition, and this perception directly affects the finest vascular vessels right into the blood circulation and respiration. The young child's physical and bodily existence is thus affected immediately by the spiritual impressions received. We may admonish a child, we may say all kinds of things, but until the seventh year this is all meaningless to the child. The only thing that matters is how we ourselves act and behave in its presence. Until the change of teeth, a child is entirely an imitating being, and upbringing and education can be effected only by setting the proper example to be imitated. This is the case for moral matters as well.

In such matters one can have some rather strange experiences. One day a father of a young child came to me in a state of great agitation because (so he told me) his son, who had always been such a good boy, had stolen! The father was very confused, because he was afraid this was a sign that his son would develop into a morally delinquent person. I said to him, "Let's examine first whether your son has really stolen. What has he actually done?" "He has taken money out of the cupboard from which his mother takes money to pay household expenses. With this money he bought sweets, which he gave to other children." I could reassure the father that his boy had not stolen at all, that the child had merely imitated what he had seen his mother do several times every day. Instinctively he had imitated his mother, taking money out of the cupboard, because Mother had been doing it.

Whether in kindergarten or at home, we educate the child only when we base all education and child rearing on the principle of imitation, which works until the second dentition. Speaking, too, is learned purely by imitation. Up to the change of teeth, a child learns everything through imitation. The only principle necessary at this stage is that human behavior should be worthy of imitation. This includes also thinking, because in their own way, children perceive whether our thoughts are moral or not. People do not usually believe in these imponderables, but they are present nevertheless. While around young children, we should not allow ourselves even a single thought that is unworthy of being absorbed by the child.

These things are all connected directly with the child as an imitator until the change of teeth. Until then all possibility of teaching and bringing up a child depends on recognizing this principle of imitation. There is no need to consider whether we should introduce one or another Froebel kindergarten method, because everything that has been contrived in this field belongs to the age of materialism. Even when we work with children according to the Froebel system, it is not the actual content of the work that influences them, but how we do it. Whatever we ask children to do without doing it first ourselves in front of them is merely extra weight that we impose on them.

The situation changes when the child's change of teeth begins. During this stage the primary principle of early educa- tion is the teacher's natural authority. Acceptance of authority is spontaneous on the child's part, and it is not necessary to enforce it in any way. During the first seven years of life a child will copy what we do. During the second seven years, from the change of teeth until puberty, a child is guided and oriented by what those in authority bring through their own conduct and through their words. This relationship has nothing to do with the role of freedom in human life in a social and individual sense, but it has everything to do with the nature of the child between the second dentition and puberty. At this point it is simply part of a child's nature to want to look up with natural respect to the authority of a revered teacher who represents all that is right and good. Between the seventh and fourteenth years, a child still cannot judge objectively whether something is true, good, or beautiful; therefore only through the guidance of a naturally respected authority can the students find their bearings in life. Advocating the elimination of a child's faith in the teacher's authority at this particular age would actually eliminate any real and true education.

Why does a child of this age believe something is true? Because the authority of the teacher and educator says so. The teacher is the source of truth. Why does something appeal to a child of this age as beautiful? Because the teacher reveals it as such. This also applies to goodness. At this age children have to gain abstract judgment of truth, goodness, and beauty by experiencing concretely the judgments of those in authority. Everything depends on whether the adult in charge exerts a self-evident authority on the child between seven and fourteen; for now the child is no longer a sense organ but has developed a soul that needs nourishment in the form of images or thoughts. We now have to introduce all teaching subjects imaginatively, pictorially—that is, artistically. To do so, teachers need the gift of bringing everything to children at this age in the form of living pictures.

As teachers, we ourselves must be able to live in a world of imagery. For example, let's imagine that we have to teach a young child to read. Consider what this implies—the child is expected to decipher signs written or printed on paper. In this form they are completely alien to the child. Sounds, speech, and vowels that carry a person's feelings and are inwardly experienced, are not alien to the child. A child knows the sense of wonder felt at seeing the sun rise. "Ah" (*A*) is the sound of wonder. The sound is there, but what does the sign that we write on paper have to do with it? The child knows the feeling of apprehension of something uncanny: "Oo" (*U*).

But what does the sign we write on the paper have to do with this sound? The child has no inner relationship to what has become modern abstract writing. If we return to earlier civilizations, we find that writing was different then. In ancient days, people painted what they wished to express. Look at

Egyptian hieroglyphics—they have a direct relationship to the human soul. When introducing writing to the child, we must return to expressing what we wish to communicate in the form of pictures. This is possible, however, only when we do not begin by introducing the alphabet directly, nor reading as a subject, but when we start with painting.

Consequently, when young students enter our school, we introduce them first to the world of flowing colors with watercolor painting. Naturally, this can cause a certain amount of chaos and disorder in the classroom, but the teacher copes with that. The children learn how to work with paints, and through the use of color the teacher can guide them toward definite forms. With the necessary skill, the teacher can allow the shapes of the letters to evolve from such painted forms. In this way, the children gain a direct relationship to the various shapes of the letters. It is possible to develop the written vowels *A* or *U* so that first one paints the mood of wonder (or of fright), finally allowing the picture to assume the form of the appropriate letters.

All teaching must have an artistic quality based on the pictorial element. The first step is to involve the whole being of the child in the effort of painting, which is subsequently transformed into writing. Only later do we develop the faculty of reading, which is linked to the head system—that is, to only one part of the human being. Reading comes after writing. First a form of drawing with paint (leading the child from color experience to form), out of which writing is evolved. Only then do we introduce reading.

The point is that, from the nature of the child, the teacher should learn how to proceed. This is the right way of finding the appropriate method, based on one's observation and knowledge of the child. Our Waldorf school has to do with method, not theory. It always endeavors to solve the wonderful riddle, the riddle of the growing child, and to introduce to the child what the child's own nature is bringing to the surface. In using this method, one finds that between the second dentition and puberty one has to approach all teaching pictorially and imaginatively, and this is certainly possible.

Yet, in order to carry the necessary authority, one has to have the right attitude toward what one's pictures really represent. For example, it is possible to speak to one's students even at a relatively early age about the immortality of the human soul. (In giving this example, I am not trying to solve a philosophical problem, but speak only from the perspective of practical pedagogy.) One could say to a child, "Look at the cocoon and its shape." One should show it to a child if possible. "You see, the cocoon opens and a butterfly flies out! This is how it is when a human being dies. The human body is like the cocoon of a butterfly. The soul flies out of the body, even though we cannot see it. When someone dies, just as the butterfly flies out of the cocoon, so the soul flies out of the body into the spiritual world."

Now, there are two possible ways that a teacher can introduce this simile. In one instance, the teacher may feel very superior to the "ignorant" student, considering oneself clever and the child ignorant. But this attitude does not accomplish much. If, in creating a picture for the child, one thinks that one is doing so only to help the child understand the abstract concept of immortality, such a picture will not convey much, because imponderables play a role. Indeed, the child will gain nothing unless the teacher is convinced of the truth of this picture, feeling that one is involved with something sacred. Those who can look into the spiritual world believe in the truth of this picture, because they know that, with the emerging butterfly, divine-spiritual powers have pictured in the world the immortality of the human soul. Such people know this image to be true and not a teacher's concoction for the benefit of "ignorant" students. If teachers feel united with this picture, believing what they have put into it and thus identifying themselves with it, they will be real and natural authorities for their students. Then the child is ready to accept much, although it will appear fruitful only later in life.

It has become popular to present everything in simple and graphic form so that "even children can understand it." This results in appalling trivialities. One thing, however, is not considered. Let's assume that, when the teacher stands before the child as the representative and source of truth, beauty, and goodness, a child of seven accepts something on the teacher's authority, knowing that the teacher believes in it. The child cannot yet understand the point in question because the necessary life experience has not occurred. Much later—say, at the age of thirty five—life may bring something like an "echo," and suddenly the former student realizes that long ago the teacher spoke about the same thing, which only now, after having gained a great deal more life experience, can be understood fully.

In this way a bridge is made between the person who was eight or nine years old, and the person who is now thirty-five years old, and this has a tremendously revitalizing effect on such a person, granting a fresh increase of life forces. This fact is well-known to anyone with a deep knowledge of the human being, and education must be built on such knowledge.

Through using our educational principles in the Waldorf school in this and similar ways, we endeavor to attune our education of body, soul, and spirit to the innermost core of the child's being. For example, there might be a phlegmatic child in a class. We pay great attention to the children's temperaments, and we even arrange the seating order in the classrooms according to temperaments. Consequently we put the phlegmatic children into one group. This is not only convenient for the teachers, because they are always aware of where their young phlegmatics are sitting, but it also has a beneficial effect on the children themselves, in that the phlegmatics who sit together bore each other to death with their indifference. By overcoming some of their temperament, they become a little more balanced.

As for the cholerics who constantly push and punch each other when sitting together, they learn in a wonderfully corrective way how to curb their temperament, at least to some extent! And so it goes. If teachers know how to deal with the various temperaments by assuming, let us say, a thoroughly phlegmatic attitude themselves when dealing with phlegmatic children, they cause in these little phlegmatics a real inner disgust with their own temperament.

Such things must become a part of our teaching, in order to turn it into a really artistic task. It is especially important for students at this age. Teachers may have a melancholic child in their class. If they can look into the spiritual background, in an anthroposophical sense, they may want to find and think through some measure for the benefit of such a child. The education we speak of begins with the knowledge that spirit exists in everything of a physical-bodily nature. One cannot see through matter, but one can learn to know it by seeing its spiritual counterpart, thereby discovering the nature of matter. Materialism suffers from ignorance of what matter really is, because it does not see the spirit in matter.

To return to our little melancholic, such a student can cause us serious concern. The teacher might feel prompted to come up with very ingenious ideas to help the child overcome a particularly melancholic temperament. This, however, can often prove fruitless. Although such a situation may have been observed very correctly, the measures taken may not lead to the desired effect. If, on the other hand, teachers realize that a deterioration of the liver function is at the root of this melancholic nature, if they suspect that there is something wrong with the child's liver, they will know the course of action necessary. They must contact the child's parents and find out as much as possible about the child's eating habits. In this way they may discover that the little melancholic needs to eat more sugar. The teachers try to win the parents' cooperation, because they know from spiritual science that the beginnings of a degeneration in the liver function connected with melancholia can be overcome by an increased sugar intake. If they succeed in gaining the parents' help, they will have taken the right step from an educational perspective. It would be necessary to know, through spiritual insight, that an increase of sugar consumption can heal or balance a pathological liver condition.

One must be able to perceive and know the growing child and even the individual organs. This is fundamental in our education. We do not insist on particular external circumstances for our schooling. Whether forest or heath, town or country, our opinion is that one can succeed in a fruitful education within any existing social conditions, as long as one really understands the human being deeply, and if, above all, one knows how the child develops.

These are only a few criteria that I may speak of today, which characterize the nature of Waldorf education and the methods used for its implementation, all of which are based on a spiritual-scientific foundation.

If one can approach the child's being in this way, the necessary strength is found to help children develop both physically and morally, so that fundamental moral forces manifest also. Barbaric forms of punishment are unnecessary, because the teacher's natural authority will ensure the proper inner connection between teacher and child. Wonderful things can happen in our Waldorf school to demonstrate this. For example, the following incident occurred a little while ago: Among our teachers there was one who imported all kinds of customary disciplinary measures from conventional school life into the Waldorf school. When a few children were naughty, he thought he would have to keep them in after school. He told them that they would have to stay behind as punishment and do some extra work in arithmetic. Spontaneously, the whole class pleaded to be allowed to stay behind and do arithmetic as well, because, as they called out, "Arithmetic is such fun!" What better things could they do than additional work in arithmetic? "We too want to be kept in," they declared. Well, here you have an example of what can happen in the Waldorf school where teachers have implanted in their students the right attitude toward work. The teacher of course had to learn his own lesson: One must never use something that should be considered a reward as a punishment. This example is one of many that could be mentioned. It shows how one can create a real art of education based on knowledge of the human being.

I am extremely thankful to Mrs. Mackenzie for giving me the opportunity of at least outlining just some of the fundamentals of education based upon anthroposophical spiritual science. Our teaching is based on definite methods, and not on vague ideals born of mere fantasy. These methods answer the needs and demands of human nature and are the primary justification for our education. We do not believe in creating ideas of what ideal human beings should be so that they fit into preconceived plans. Our goal is to be able to observe children realistically, to hear the message sent to us through the children from the divine-spiritual worlds. We wish to feel the children's inner affirmation of our picture of the human being. God, speaking through the child, says: "This is how I wish to become."

We try to fulfil this call for the child through our educational methods in the best way possible. Through our art of education, we try to supply a positive answer to this call.

12

Educational Issues

LONDON — AUGUST 30, 1924

PART TWO

First I must thank Mrs. MacMillan and Mrs. Mackenzie for their kind words of greeting and for the beautiful way they have introduced our theme. Furthermore, I must apologize for speaking to you in German followed by an English translation. I know that this will make your understanding more difficult, but it is something I cannot avoid.

What I have to tell you is not about general ideas on educational reform or formalized programs of education; basically, it is about the practice of teaching, which stands the test of time only when actually applied in classroom situations. This teaching has been practiced in the Waldorf school for several years now. It has shown tangible and noticeable results, and it has been recognized in England also; on the strength of this, it became possible, through the initiative of Mrs. Mackenzie, for me to give educational lectures in Oxford. This form of teaching is the result not only of what must be called a spiritual view of the world, but also of spiritual research. Spiritual research leads first to a knowledge of human nature, and, through that, to a knowledge of the "human being becoming," from early childhood until death. This form of spiritual research is possible only when one acknowledges that the human being can look into the spiritual world when the necessary and relevant forces of cognition are developed. It is difficult to present in a short survey of this vast theme what normally needs to be acquired through a specific training of the human soul, with the goal of acquiring the faculty of perceiving and comprehending not just the material aspects of the human being and the sensory world, but also the spiritual element, so that this spiritual element may work in the human will.

However, I will certainly try to indicate what I mean. One can strengthen and intensify inner powers of the soul, just as it is possible to research the sense-perceptible world by external experiments using instrumental aids such as the microscope, telescope, or other optical devices, through which the sense world yields more of its secrets and reveals more to our vision than in ordinary circumstances. By forging inner "soul instruments" in this way, it is possible to perceive the spiritual world in its own right through the soul's own powers. One can then discover also the fuller nature of the human being, that what is generally understood of the human being in ordinary consciousness and through the so-called sciences is only a small part of the whole of human nature, and that beyond the physical aspect, a second human being exists.

As I begin to describe this, remember that names do not matter, but we must have them. I make use of old names because they are known here and there from literature. Nevertheless, I must ask you not to be put off by these names. They do not stem from superstition, but from exact research. Nevertheless, there is no reason why one should not use other names instead. In any case, the second human member, which I shall call the *etheric body,* is visible when one's soul forces have been sufficiently strengthened as a means for a deeper cognition (just as the physical senses, by means of microscope or telescope, can penetrate more deeply into the sense world). This *etheric body* is the first of the spiritual bodies linked with the human physical body.

When studying the physical human being only from the viewpoint of conventional science, one cannot really understand how the physical body of the human being can exist throughout a lifetime. This is because, in reality, most physical substances in the body disappear within a period of seven to eight years. No one sitting here is the same, physically speaking, as the person of some seven or eight years ago! The substances that made up the body then have in the meantime been cast off, and new ones have taken their place. In the etheric body we have the first real supersensible entity, which rules and permeates us with forces of growth and nourishment throughout earthly life.

The ether body is the first supersensible body to consider. The human being has an ether body, just as plants do, but minerals do not. The only thing we have in common with the minerals is a physical form. However, furnished with those specially developed inner senses and perceptions developed by powers of the soul, we come to recognize also a third sheath or member of the human being, which we call the *astral body*. (Again I must ask you not to be disturbed by the name.) The human being has an astral body, as do animals. We experience sensation through the astral body. An organism such as the plant, which can grow and nourish itself, does not need sensation, but human beings and animals can sense. The astral body cannot be designated by an abstract word, because it is a reality.

And then we find something that makes the human being into a bearer of three bodies, an entity that controls the physical, etheric, and astral bodies. It is the *I*, the real inner spiritual core the human being. So the four members are first the physical body, second the etheric body, third the astral body, and finally the human I-organization.

Let those who are not aware of these four members of the human being—those who believe that external observation, such as in anatomy and physiology, encompasses the entire human being—try to find a world view! It is possible to formulate ideas in many ways, whether or not they are accepted by the world. Accordingly one may be a spiritualist, an idealist, a materialist, or a realist. It is not difficult to establish views of the world, because one only needs to formulate them verbally; one only needs to maintain a belief in one or another viewpoint. But unless one's world views stem from actual realities and from real observations and experiences, they are of no use for dealing with the external aspect of the human being, nor for education.

Let's suppose you are a bridge builder and base your mechanical construction on a faulty principle: the bridge will collapse as the first train crosses it. When working with mechanics, realistic or unrealistic assumptions will prove right or wrong immediately. The same is true in practical life when dealing with human beings. It is very possible to digest world views from treatises or books, but one cannot educate on this basis; it is only possible to do so on the strength of a real knowledge of the human being. This kind of knowledge is what I want to speak about, because it is the only real preparation for the teaching profession. All external knowledge that, no matter how ingeniously contrived, tells a teacher what to do and how to do it, is far less important than the teacher's ability to look into human nature itself and, from a love for education and the art of education, allow the child's own nature to tell the teacher how and what to teach.

Even with this knowledge, however—a knowledge strengthened by supersensible perception of the human being—we will find it impossible during the first seven years of the child's life, from birth to the second dentition, to differentiate between the four human members or sheaths of which I have just spoken. One cannot say that the young child consists of physical body, etheric body, astral body and I, in the same way as in the case of an adult. Why not?

A newborn baby is truly the greatest wonder to be found in all earthly life. Anyone who is open-minded is certain to experience this. A child enters the world with a still unformed physiognomy, an almost "neutral" physiognomy, and with jerky and uncoordinated movements. We may feel, possibly with a sense of superiority, that a baby is not yet suited to live in this world, that it is not yet fit for earthly experience. The child lacks the primitive skill of grasping objects properly; it cannot yet focus its eyes properly, cannot express the dictates of the will through limb movement. One of the most sublime experiences is to see gradually evolve, out of the central core of human nature, out of inner forces, that which gives the physiognomy its godlike features, what coordinates the limb movements to suit outer conditions, and so on. And yet, if one observes the child from a supersensible perspective, one cannot say that the child has a physical, etheric, and astral body plus an I, just as one cannot say that water in its natural state is composed of hydrogen and oxygen. Water does consist of hydrogen and oxygen, but these two elements are most intimately fused together. Similarly, in the child's organism until the change of teeth, the four human members are so intimately merged together that for the time being it is impossible to differentiate between them.

Only with the change of teeth, around the seventh year, when children enter primary education, does the etheric body come into its own as the basis of growth, nutrition, and so on; it is also the basis for imagination, for the forces of mind and soul, and for the forces of love. If one observes a child of seven with supersensible vision, it is as if a supersensible etheric cloud were emerging, containing forces that were as yet little in control because, prior to the change of teeth, they were still deeply embedded in the physical organism and accustomed to working homogeneously within the physical body. With the coming of the second teeth they become freer to work more independently, sending down into the physical body only a portion of their forces. The surplus then works in the processes of growth, nutrition, and so on, but also has free reign in supporting the child's life of imagination. These etheric forces do not yet work in the intellectual sphere, in thinking or ideas, but they want to appear on a higher level than the physical in a love for things and in a love for human beings. The soul has become free in the child's etheric body. Having gone through the change of teeth the child, basically, has become a different being.

Now another life period begins, from the change of teeth until puberty. When the child reaches sexual maturity, the astral body, which so far could be differentiated only very little, emerges. One notices that the child gains a different relationship to the outer world. The more the astral body is born, the greater the change in the child. Previously it was as if the astral body were embedded in the physical and etheric organization.

Thus to summarize: First, physical birth occurs when the embryo leaves the maternal body. Second, the etheric body is born when the child's own etheric body wrests itself free. Due to the emergence of the etheric body we can begin to teach the child. Third, the astral body emerges with the coming of puberty, which enables the adolescent to develop a loving interest in the outside world and to experience the differences between human beings, because sexual maturity is linked not only with an awakening of sexual love, but also with a knowledge gained through the adolescent's immersion in all aspects of life. Fourth, I-consciousness is born only in the twenty-first or twenty-second year. Only then does the human being become an independent I-being.

Thus, when speaking about the human being from a spiritual perspective, one can speak of four successive births. Only when one knows the condition of the human being under the influence of these successively developing members, can one adequately guide the education and training of children. For what does it mean if, prior to the change of teeth, the physical body, the etheric body, the astral body, and the I cannot yet be differentiated? It means that they are merged, like hydrogen and oxygen in water. This, in turn, means that the child really is as yet entirely a sense organ. Everything is related to the child in the same way a sense impression is related to the sense organ; whatever the child absorbs, is absorbed as in a sense organ.

Look at the wonderful creation of the human eye. The whole world is reflected within the eye in images. We can say that the world is both outside and inside the eye. In the young child we have the same situation; the world is out there, and the world is also within the child. The child is entirely a sense organ. We adults taste sugar in the mouth, tongue, and palate. The child is entirely permeated by the taste. One only needs eyes to observe that the child is an organ of taste through and through. When looking at the world, the child's whole being partakes of this activity, is surrendered to the visible surroundings. Consequently a characteristic trait follows in children; they are naturally pious. Children surrender to parents and educators in the same way that the eye surrenders to the world. If the eye could see itself, it could not see anything else. Children live entirely in the environment. They also absorb impressions physically.

Let's take the case of a father with a disposition to anger and to sudden outbursts of fury, who lives closely with a child. He does all kinds of things, and his anger is expressed in his gestures. The child perceives these gestures very differently than one might imagine. The young child perceives in these gestures also the father's moral quality. What the child sees inwardly is bathed in a moral light. In this way the child is inwardly saturated by the outbursts of an angry father, by the gentle love of a mother, or by the influence of anyone else nearby. This affects the child, even into the physical body.

Our being, as adults, enters a child's being just as the candle-light enters the eye. Whatever we are around a child spreads its influence so that the child's blood circulates differently in the sense organs and in the nerves; since these operate differently in the muscles and vascular liquids which nourish them, the entire being of the child is transformed according to the external sense impressions received. One can notice the effect that the moral and religious environment of childhood has had on an old person, including the physical constitution. A child's future condition of health and illness depends on our ability to realize deeply enough that everything in the child's environment is mirrored in the child. The physical element, as well as the moral element, is reflected and affects a person's health or illness later.

During the first seven years, until the change of teeth, children are purely imitative beings. We should not preconceive what they should do. We must simply act for them what we want them to do. The only healthy way to teach children of this age is to do in front of them what we wish them to copy. Whatever we do in their presence will be absorbed by their physical organs. And children will not learn anything unless we do it in front of them.

In this respect one can have some interesting experiences. Once a father came to me because he was very upset. He told me that his five-year-old child had stolen. He said to me, "This child will grow into a dreadful person, because he has stolen already at this tender age." I replied, "Let us first discover whether the boy has really stolen." And what did we find? The boy had taken money out of the chest of drawers from which his mother habitually took money whenever she needed it for the household. The mother was the very person whom the boy imitated most. To the child it was a matter of course to do what his mother did, and so he too took money from the drawer. There was no question of his thieving, for he only did what was natural for a child below the age of the second dentition: he imitated. He only imitated what his mother had done.

When this example is understood, one knows that, in the case of young children, imitation is the thing that rules their physical and soul development. As educators we must realize that during these first seven years we adults are instrumental in developing the child's body, soul, and spirit. Education and upbringing during these first seven years must be formative. If one can see through this situation properly, one can recognize in people's physiognomy, in their gait, and in their other habits, whether as children they were surrounded by anger or by kindness and gentleness, which, working into the blood formation and circulation, and into the individual character of the muscular system, have left lasting marks on the person. Body, soul, and spirit are formed during these years, and as teachers we must know that this is so. Out of this knowledge and impulse, and out of the teacher's ensuing enthusiasm, the appropriate methods and impulses of feeling and will originate in one's teaching. An attitude of dedication and self-sacrifice has to be the foundation of educational methods. The most beautiful pedagogical ideas are without value unless they have grown out of knowledge of the child and unless the teachers can grow along with their students, to the extent that the children may safely imitate them, thus recreating the teachers' qualities in their own being.

For the reasons mentioned, I would like to call the education of the child until the change of teeth "formative education," because everything is directed toward forming the child's body, soul, and spirit for all of earthly life. One only has to look carefully at this process of formation. I have quoted the example of an angry father. In the gesture of a passionate temperament, the child perceives inherent moral or immoral qualities. These affect the child so that they enter the physical constitution. It may happen that a fifty-year-old person begins to develop cataracts in the eyes and needs an operation. These things are accepted and seen only from the present medical perspective. It looks as if there is a cataract, and this is the way to treat it, and there the matter ends; the preceding course of life is not considered. If one were ready to do that, it would be found that a cataract can often be traced back to the inner shocks experienced by the young child of an angry father. In such cases, what is at work in the moral and religious sphere of the environment spreads its influence into the bodily realm, right down to the vascular system, eventually leading to health or illness. This often surfaces only later in life, and the doctor then makes a diagnosis based on current circumstances. In reality, we are led back to the fact that, for example, gout or rheumatism at the age of fifty or sixty can be linked to an attitude of carelessness, untidiness, or disharmony that ruled the environment of such a patient during childhood. These circumstances were absorbed by the child and entered the organic sphere.

If one observes what a child has absorbed during the stage of imitation up to the change of teeth, one can recognize that the human being at this time is molded for the whole of life. Unless we learn to direct rightly the formative powers in the young human being, all our early childhood education is without value. We must allow for germination of the forces that control health and illness for all of earthly life.

With the change of teeth, the etheric body emerges, controlling the forces of digestion, nutrition, and growth, and it begins to manifest in the realm of the soul through the faculty of fantasy, memory, and so on. We must be clear about what we are educating during the years between the second dentition and puberty. What are we educating in the child during this period? We are working with the same forces that effect proper digestion and enable the child to grow. They are transformed forces of growth, working freely now within the soul realm. What do nature and the spiritual world give to the human being through the etheric body's forces of growth? Life—actual life itself! Since we cannot bestow life directly as nature does during the first seven years, and since it is our task to work on the liberated etheric body in the soul realm, what should we, as teachers, give the child? We should give life! But we cannot do this if, at such an early stage, we introduce finished concepts to the child. The child is not mature enough yet for intellectual work, but is mature enough for imagery, for imagination, and for memory training. With the recognition of what needs to be done at this age, one knows that everything taught must have the breath of life. Everything needs to be enlivened. Between the change of teeth and puberty, the appropriate principle is to bestow life through all teaching. Everything the teacher does, must enliven the student. However, at just this age, it is really too easy to bring death with one's teaching.

As correctly demanded by civilization, our children must be taught reading and writing. But now consider how alien and strange the letters of the alphabet are to a child. In themselves letters are so abstract and obscure that, when the Europeans, those so-called superior people, came to America (examples of this exist from the 1840s), the Native Americans said: "These Europeans use such strange signs on paper. They look at them and then they put what is written on paper into words. These signs are little devils!" Thus said the Native Americans: "The Palefaces [as they called the Europeans] use these little demons." For the young child, just as for the Indians, the letters are little demons, for the child has no immediate relationship to them.

If we introduce reading abstractly right away, we kill a great deal in the child. This makes no sense to anyone who can see through these matters. Consequently, educational principles based on a real knowledge of the human being will refer to the ancient Egyptian way of writing. They still put down what they had actually seen, making a picture of it. These hieroglyphics gave rise to our present letters. The ancient Egyptians did not write letters, they painted pictures. Cuneiform writing has a similar origin. In Sanskrit writing one can still see how the letters came from pictures. You must remember that this is the path humanity has gone on its way to modern abstract letters, to which we no longer have an immediate relationship. What then can we do? The solution is to not plague children at all with writing and reading from the time they begin school. Instead, we have them draw and paint. When we guide children in color and form by painting, the whole body participates. We let children paint the forms and shapes of what they see. Then the pictures are guided into the appropriate sounds.

Let's take, for example, the English word *fish*. By combining the activity of painting and drawing with a brush, the child manages to make a picture of a fish. Now we can ask the child to pronounce the word *fish*, but very slowly. After this, one could say, "Now sound only the beginning of the word: 'F.'" In this way the letter *F* emerges from the picture that was painted of the fish. One can proceed in a similar way with all consonant sounds. With the vowels, one can lead from the picture to the letters by taking examples from a person's inner life of feeling.

In this way, beginning at the age of seven or eight, children learn a combined form of painting and drawing. Teachers can hardly relax during this activity, because painting lessons with young children inevitably create a big mess, which always has to be cleaned up at the end of the lesson. Yet this inconvenience must be carried by the teacher with understanding and equanimity. The first step is for the children to learn to create resemblances of outer shapes, using color and form. This leads to writing. In learning to write, the child brings the whole body into movement, not just one part. Only the head is involved when we read, which is the third step, after writing. This happens around the ninth year, when the child learns to read through the activity of writing, which was developed from painting.

In doing this, the child's nature gives us the cue, and the child's nature always directs us in how to proceed. This means that teachers are forced to become different human beings. They can't learn their lessons and then apply them abstractly; they must instead stand before the class as whole human beings, and for everything they do, they must find images; they must cultivate their imagination. The teachers can then communicate their intentions to the students in imperceptible ways. The teachers themselves have to be alert and alive. They will reach the child to the extent that they can offer imaginative pictures instead of abstract concepts.

It is even possible to bring moral and religious concepts through the medium of pictures. Let us assume that teachers wish to speak to children about the immortality of the human soul. They could speak about the butterfly hidden in a chrysalis. A small hole appears in the chrysalis, and the butterfly emerges. Teachers could talk to children as follows: The butterfly, emerging from the chrysalis, shows you what happens when a person dies. While alive, the person is like the chrysalis. The soul, like the butterfly, flies out of the body only at death. The butterfly is visible when it leaves the chrysalis. Although we cannot see the soul with our eyes when a person dies, it nevertheless flies into the spiritual world like a butter-fly from the chrysalis.

There are, however, two ways teachers can proceed. If they feel inwardly superior to the children, they will not succeed in using this simile. They may think they are very smart and that the children's ignorance forces them to invent something that gets the idea of immortality across, while they themselves do not believe this butterfly and chrysalis "humbug," and consider it only a useful ploy. As a result they fail to make any lasting impression on the children; for here, in the depths of the soul, forces work between teacher and child. If I, as the teacher, believe that spiritual forces in nature, operating at the level of the newly-emerged butterfly, provide an image of immortality, if I am fully alive in this image of the butterfly emerging from the chrysalis, then my comparison will work strongly on the child's soul. This simile will work like a seed, and grow prop-erly in the child, working beneficently on the soul. This is an example of how we can keep our concepts mobile, because it would be the greatest mistake to approach a child directly with frozen intellectual concepts.

If one buys new shoes for a three-year-old, one would hardly expect the child to still be wearing them at nine. The child would then need different, larger shoes. And yet, when it comes to teaching young children, people often act exactly like this, expecting the student to retain unchanged, possibly until the age of forty or fifty, what was learned at a young age. They tend to give definitions, meant to remain unchanged like the metaphorical shoes given to a child of three, as if the child would not outgrow their usefulness later in life! The point is that, when educating we must allow the soul to grow according to the demands of nature and the growing physical body. Teachers can give a child living concepts that grow with the human being only when they acquire the necessary liveliness to permeate all their teaching with imagination.

We need education that enlivens the human being during the years between the change of teeth and puberty. The etheric body can then become free. For example, take the word *mouth*. If I pronounce only the first letter, "M," I can transform this line as picture of a mouth to this:

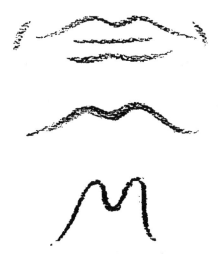

Similarly, I can find other ways to use living pictures to bridge the gap to written letters of the alphabet. Then, if the intellect (which is meant to be developed only at puberty) is not called on too soon, the ideas born out of the teacher's imagination will grow with the child. Definitions are poison to the child. This always brings to mind a definition that once was made in a Greek philosophers' school. The question, "What is a human being?" received the answer, "A human being is a creature with two legs and no feathers." The following day, a student of the school brought a goose whose feathers had been plucked out, maintaining that this was a human being—a creature with two legs and without feathers. (Incidentally, this type of definition can sometimes be found in contemporary scientific literature. I know that in saying this I am speaking heresy, but roughly speaking, this is the kind of intellectual concept we often offer children.)

We need rich, imaginative concepts, that can grow with the child, concepts that allow growth forces to remain active even when a person reaches old age. If children are taught only abstract concepts, they will display signs of aging early in life. We lose fresh spontaneity and stop making human progress. It is a terrifying experience when we realize we have not grown up with fantasy, with images, with pictures that grow and live and are suited to the etheric body, but instead we grew up merely with those suited to abstraction, to intellectualism—that is, to death.

When we recognize that the etheric body really exists, that it is a living reality—when we know it not just in theory but from observing a developing child—then we will experience the second golden principle of education, engraved in our hearts. The golden principle during the first seven years is: *Mold the child's being in a manner worthy of human imitation, and thus cultivate the child's health.* During the second seven years, from the change of teeth to puberty, the guiding motive or principle of education should be: *Enliven the students, because their etheric bodies have been entrusted to your care.*

With the coming of puberty, what I have called the astral body is freed in a new kind of birth. This is the very force that, during the age of primary education until the beginning of puberty, was at the base of the child's inmost human forces, in the life of feeling. This force then lived undifferentiated within the latent astral body, still undivided from the physical and etheric bodies. This spiritual aggregate is entrusted to the quality of the teachers' imaginative handling, and to their sensitive feeling and tact. As the child's astral body is gradually liberated from the physical organization, becoming free to work in the soul realm, the child is also freed from what previously had to be present as a natural faith in the teacher's authority. What I described earlier as the only appropriate form of education between the change of teeth and puberty has to come under the auspices of a teacher's natural authority.

Oh! It is such great fortune for all of life when, at just this age, children can look up to their teachers as people who wield natural authority, so that what is truth for the teacher, is also very naturally truth to the students. Children cannot, out of their own powers, discriminate between something true and something false. They respect as truth what the teacher calls the truth. Because the teacher opens the child's eyes to goodness, the child respects goodness. The child finds truth, goodness, and beauty in the world through venerating the personality of the teacher.

Surely no one expects that I, who, many years ago, wrote *Intuitive Thinking as a Spiritual Path: A Philosophy of Freedom*, would stand for the principle of authoritarianism in social life. I am saying here that the child, between the second dentition and puberty, has to experience the feeling of a natural authority from the adults in charge, and that, during these years, everything the student receives must be truly alive. The educator must be the unquestioned authority at this age, because the human being is ready for freedom only after having learned to respect and venerate the natural authority of a teacher. Only after reaching sexual maturity, when the astral body has become the means for individual judgments, can the student form judgments instead of accepting those of the teacher.

Now what must be considered the third principle of education comes into its own. The first one I called "the formative element," the second one "the enlivening element." The third element of education, which enters with puberty, can be properly called "an awakening education." Everything taught after puberty must affect adolescents so that their emerging independent judgment appears as a continual awakening. If one attempts to drill subjects into a student who has reached puberty, one tyrannizes the adolescent, making the student into a slave. If, on the other hand, one's teaching is arranged so that, from puberty on, adolescents receive their subject matter as if they were being awakened from a sleep, they learn to depend on their own judgments, because with regard to making their own judgments, they were indeed asleep. The students should now feel they are calling on their own individuality, and all education, all teaching, will be perceived as a stimulus and awakener. This can be realized when teachers have proceeded as I have indicated for the first two life periods. This last stage in education will then have a quality of awakening. And if in their style, posture, and presentation, teachers demonstrate that they are themselves permeated with the quality of awakening, their teaching will be such that what must come from those learning will truly come from them. The process should reach a kind of dramatic intensification when adolescents inwardly join with active participation in the lessons, an activity that proceeds very particularly from the astral body.

Appealing properly in this way to the astral body, we address the immortal being of the student. The physical body is renewed and exchanged every seven years. The etheric body gives its strength as a dynamic force and lasts from birth, or conception, until death. What later emerges as the astral body represents, as already mentioned, the eternal kernel of the human being, which descends to Earth, enveloping itself with the sheaths of the physical and etheric bodies before passing again through the portal of death. We address this astral body properly only when, during the two previous life periods, we have related correctly to the child's etheric and physical bodies, which the human being receives only as an Earth dweller. If we have educated the child as described so far, the eternal core of the human individuality, which is to awaken at puberty, develops in an inwardly miraculous way, not through our guidance, but through the guidance of the spiritual world itself.

Then we may confidently say to ourselves that we have taken the right path in educating children, because we did not force the subject matter on them; neither did we dictate our own attitude to them, because we were content to remove the hurdles and obstacles from the way so that their eternal core could enter life openly and freely. And now, during the last stage, our education must take the form of awakening the students. We make our stand in the school saying, "We are the cultivators of the divine-spiritual world order; we are its collaborators and want to nurture the eternal in the human being." We must be able to say this to ourselves or feel ashamed. Perhaps, sitting there among our students are one or two geniuses who will one day know much more than we teachers ever will. And what we as teachers can do to justify working with students, who one day may far surpass us in soul and spirit, and possibly also in physical strength, is to say to ourselves: Only when we nurture spirit and soul in the child—*nurture* is the word, not *overpower*—only when we aid the development of the seed planted in the child by the divine-spiritual world, only when we become "spiritual midwives," then we will have acted correctly as teachers. We can accomplish this by working as described, and our insight into human nature will guide us in the task.

Having listened to my talk about the educational methods of the Waldorf school, you may wonder whether they imply that all teachers there have the gift of supersensible insight, and whether they can observe the births of the etheric and astral bodies. Can they really observe the unfolding of human forces in their students with the same clarity investigators use in experimental psychology or science to observe outer phenomena with the aid of a microscope? The answer is that certainly not every teacher in the Waldorf school has developed sufficient clairvoyant powers to see these things with inward eyes, but it isn't necessary. If we know what spiritual research can tell us about the human being's physical, etheric, and astral bodies and about the human I-organization, we need only to use our healthy soul powers and common sense, not just to understand what the spiritual investigator is talking about, but also to comprehend all its weight and significance.

We often come across very strange attitudes, especially these days. I once gave a lecture that was publicly criticized afterward. In this lecture I said that the findings of a clairvoyant person's investigations can be understood by anyone of sane mind who is free of bias. I meant this literally, and not in any superstitious sense. I meant that a clairvoyant person can see the supersensible in the human being just as others can see the sense-perceptible in outer nature. The reply was, "This is what Rudolf Steiner asserted, but evidently it cannot be true, because if someone maintains that a supersensible spiritual world exists and that one can recognize it, one cannot be of sane mind; and if one is of sane mind, one does not make such an assertion...." Here you can see the state of affairs in our materialist age, but it has to be overcome.

Not every Waldorf teacher has the gift of clairvoyance, but every one of them has accepted wholeheartedly and with full understanding the results of spiritual-scientific investigation concerning the human being. And each Waldorf teacher applies this knowledge with heart and soul, because the child is the greatest teacher, and while one cares for the child, witnessing the wonderful development daily, weekly, and yearly, nothing can awaken the teacher more to the needs of education. In educating the child, in the daily lessons, and in the daily social life at school, the teachers find the confirmation for what spiritual science can tell them about practical teaching. Every day they grow into their tasks with increasing inner clarity. In this way, education and teaching in the Waldorf school are life itself. The school is an organism, and the teaching faculty is its soul, which, in the classrooms, in regular common study, and in the daily cooperative life within the school organism, radiates care for the individual lives of the students in all the classes.

This is how we see the possibility of carrying into our civilization what human nature itself demands in these three stages of education—the formative education before the change of teeth, the life-giving education between the change of teeth and puberty, and the awakening education after puberty, leading students into full life, which itself increasingly awakens the human individuality.

Formative education—before the change of teeth.
Life-giving education—between the change of teeth and
                        puberty.
Awakening education—after puberty.

When we look at the child properly, the following thoughts may stimulate us: In our teaching and educating we should really become priests, because what we meet in children reveals to us, in the form of outer reality and in the strongest, grandest, and most intense ways, the divine-spiritual world order that is at the foundation of outer physical, material existence. In children we see, revealed in matter in a most sublime way, what the creative spiritual powers are carrying behind the outer material world. We have been placed next to children in order that spirit properly germinates, grows, and bears fruit. This attitude of reverence must underlie every method. The most rational and carefully planned methods make sense only when seen in this light. Indeed, when our methods are illuminated by the light of these results, the children will come alive as soon as the teacher enters the classroom. Teaching will then become the most important leaven and the most important impulse in our present stage of evolution. Those who can clearly see the present time with its tendency toward decadence and decline know how badly our civilization needs revitalization.

School life and education can be the most revitalizing force. Society should therefore take hold of them in their spiritual foundations; society should begin with the human being as its fundamental core. If we start with the child, we can provide society and humanity with what the signs of the times demand from us in our present stage of civilization, for the benefit of the immediate future.

FURTHER READING

Basic Works by Rudolf Steiner

Anthroposophy (A Fragment), Anthroposophic Press, Hudson, NY, 1996.

An Autobiography, Steinerbooks, Blauvelt, NY, 1977.

Christianity as Mystical Fact, Anthroposophic Press, Hudson, NY, 1986.

How to Know Higher Worlds: A Modern Path of Initiation, Anthroposophic Press, Hudson, NY, 1994.

Intuitive Thinking as a Spiritual Path: A Philosophy of Freedom, Anthroposophic Press, Hudson, NY, 1995.

An Outline of Occult Science, Anthroposophic Press, Hudson, NY, 1972.

A Road to Self-Knowledge and The Threshold of the Spiritual World, Rudolf Steiner Press, London, 1975.

Theosophy: An Introduction to the Spiritual Processes in Human Life and in the Cosmos, Anthroposophic Press, Hudson, NY, 1994.

Books by Other Authors

Anschütz, Marieke. *Children and Their Temperaments*, Floris Books, Edinburgh, 1995.

Carlgren, Frans. *Education Towards Freedom: Rudolf Steiner Education: A Survey of the Work of Waldorf Schools throughout the World*. Lanthorn Press, East Grinstead, England, 1993.

Childs, Gilbert. *Understanding Your Temperament! A Guide to the Four Temperaments*. Sophia Books, London, 1995.

Childs, Dr. Gilbert and Sylvia Childs. *Your Reincarnating Child*. Sophia Books/Rudolf Steiner Press, London, 1995.

Edmunds, L. Francis. *Renewing Education: Selected Writings on Steiner Education*. Hawthorn Press, Stroud, UK, 1992.

——*Rudolf Steiner Education: The Waldorf School*. Rudolf Steiner Press, London, 1992.

Finser, Torin M. *School as a Journey: The Eight-Year Odyssey of a Waldorf Teacher and His Class.* Anthroposophic Press, Hudson, NY, 1994.

Gabert, Erich. *Educating the Adolescent: Discipline or Freedom.* Anthroposophic Press, Hudson, NY, 1988.

Gardner, John Fentress. *Education in Search of the Spirit: Essays on American Education.* Anthroposophic Press, Hudson, NY, 1996.

Gatto, John Taylor. *Dumbing Us Down: The Hidden Curriculum of Compulsory Schooling.* New Society, Philadelphia, 1992.

Harwood, A. C. *The Recovery of Man in Childhood: A Study in the Educational Work of Rudolf Steiner.* The Myrin Institute of New York, New York, 1992.

Heydebrand, Caroline von. *Childhood: A Study of the Growing Child,* Anthroposophic Press, Hudson, NY, 1995.

Large, Martin. *Who's Bringing Them Up? How to Break the T.V. Habit!* Hawthorn Press, Stroud, UK, 1990.

Richards, M. C. *Opening Our Moral Eye.* Lindisfarne Press, Hudson, NY, 1996.

Spock, Marjorie. *Teaching as a Lively Art.* Anthroposophic Press, Hudson, NY, 1985.

THE FOUNDATIONS
OF WALDORF EDUCATION

THE FIRST FREE WALDORF SCHOOL opened its doors in Stuttgart, Germany, in September, 1919, under the auspices of Emil Molt, the Director of the Waldorf Astoria Cigarette Company and a student of Rudolf Steiner's spiritual science and particularly of Steiner's call for social renewal.

It was only the previous year—amid the social chaos following the end of World War I—that Emil Molt, responding to Steiner's prognosis that truly human change would not be possible unless a sufficient number of people received an education that developed the whole human being, decided to create a school for his workers' children. Conversations with the Minister of Education and with Rudolf Steiner, in early 1919, then led rapidly to the forming of the first school.

Since that time, more than six hundred schools have opened around the globe—from Italy, France, Portugal, Spain, Holland, Belgium, Great Britain, Norway, Finland, and Sweden to Russia, Georgia, Poland, Hungary, Romania, Israel, South Africa, Australia, Brazil, Chile, Peru, Argentina, Japan, and others—making the Waldorf School Movement the largest independent school movement in the world. The United States, Canada, and Mexico alone now have more than 120 schools.

Although each Waldorf school is independent, and although there is a healthy oral tradition going back to the first Waldorf teachers and to Steiner himself, as well as a growing body of secondary literature, the true foundations of the Waldorf method and spirit remain the many lectures that Rudolf Steiner gave on the subject. For five years (1919–24), Rudolf Steiner, while simultaneously working on many other fronts, tirelessly dedicated himself to the dissemination of the idea of Waldorf education. He gave manifold lectures to teachers, parents, the general public, and even the children themselves. New schools were founded. The Movement grew.

While many of Steiner's foundational lectures have been translated and published in the past, some have never appeared in English, and many have been virtually unobtainable for years. To remedy this situation and to establish a coherent basis for Waldorf education, Anthroposophic Press has decided to publish the complete series of Steiner lectures and writings on education in a uniform series. This series will thus constitute an authoritative foundation for work in educational renewal, for Waldorf teachers, parents, and educators generally.

RUDOLF STEINER'S LECTURES

(AND WRITINGS) ON EDUCATION

I. *Allgemeine Menschenkunde als Grundlage der Pädagogik. Pädagogischer Grundkurs,* 14 Lectures, Stuttgart, 1919 (GA 293). Previously *Study of Man.* **Foundations of Human Experience** (Anthroposophic Press, 1996).

II. *Erziehungskunst Methodische-Didaktisches,* 14 Lectures, Stuttgart, 1919 (GA 294). **Practical Advice to Teachers** (Rudolf Steiner Press, 1988).

III. *Erziehungskunst,* 15 Discussions, Stuttgart, 1919 (GA 295). **Discussions with Teachers** (Rudolf Steiner Press, 1992).

IV. *Die Erziehungsfrage als soziale Frage,* 6 Lectures, Dornach, 1919 (GA 296). **Education as a Social Problem** (Anthroposophic Press, 1969).

V. *Die Waldorf Schule und ihr Geist,* 6 Lectures, Stuttgart and Basel, 1919 (GA 297). **The Spirit of the Waldorf School** (Anthroposophic Press, 1995).

VI. *Rudolf Steiner in der Waldorfschule, Vorträge und Ansprachen,* Stuttgart, 1919–1924 (GA 298). **Rudolf Steiner in the Waldorf School—Lectures and Conversations** (Anthroposophic Press, 1996).

VII. *Geisteswissenschaftliche Sprachbetrachtungen,* 6 Lectures, Stuttgart, 1919 (GA 299). **The Genius of Language** (Anthroposophic Press, 1995).

VIII. *Konferenzen mit den Lehren der Freien Waldorfschule 1919–1924,* 3 Volumes (GA 300). **Conferences with Teachers** (Steiner Schools Fellowship, 1986, 1987, 1988, 1989).

IX. *Die Erneuerung der Pädagogisch-didaktischen Kunst durch Geisteswissenschaft,* 14 Lectures, Basel, 1920 (GA 301). **The Renewal of Education** (Kolisko Archive Publications for Steiner Schools Fellowship Publications, Michael Hall, Forest Row, East Sussex, UK, 1981).

X. *Menschenerkenntnis und Unterrichtsgestaltung,* 8 Lectures, Stuttgart, 1921 (GA 302). Previously *The Supplementary Course—Upper School* and *Waldorf Education for Adolescence.* **Education for Adolescence** (Anthroposophic Press, 1996).

XI. *Erziehung und Unterrricht aus Menschenerkenntnis,* 9 Lectures, Stuttgart, 1920, 1922, 1923 (GA 302a). The first four lectures available as **Balance in Teaching** (Mercury Press, 1982); last three lectures as **Deeper Insights into Education** (Anthroposophic Press, 1988).

XII. *Die Gesunder Entwicklung des Menschenwesens,* 16 Lectures, Dornach, 1921–22 (GA 303). **Soul Economy and Waldorf Education** (Anthroposophic Press, 1986).

XIII. *Erziehungs- und Unterrichtsmethoden auf Anthroposophischer Grundlage,* 9 Public Lectures, various cities, 1921–22 (GA 304). **Waldorf Education and Anthroposophy 1** (Anthroposophic Press, 1995).

XIV. *Anthroposophische Menschenkunde und Pädagogik,* 9 Public Lectures, various cities, 1923–24 (GA 304a). **Waldorf Education and Anthroposophy 2** (Anthroposophic Press, 1996).

XV. *Die geistig-seelischen Grundkräfte der Erziehungskunst,* 12 Lectures, 1 Special Lecture, Oxford 1922 (GA 305). **The Spiritual Ground of Education** (Garber Publications, n.d.).

XVI. *Die pädagogisch Praxis vom Gesichtspunkte geisteswissenschaftlicher Menschenerkenntnis,* 8 Lectures, Dornach, 1923 (GA 306). **The Child's Changing Consciousness as the Basis of Pedagogical Practice** (Anthroposophic Press, 1996).

XVII. *Gegenwärtiges Geistesleben und Erziehung,* 4 Lectures, Ilkley, 1923 (GA 307). **A Modern Art of Education** (Rudolf Steiner Press, 1981) and **Education and Modern Spiritual Life** (Garber Publications, n.d.).

XVIII. *Die Methodik des Lehrens und die Lebensbedingungen des Erziehens,* 5 Lectures, Stuttgart, 1924 (GA 308). **The Essentials of Education** (Rudolf Steiner Press, 1968).

XIX. *Anthroposophische Pädagogik und ihre Voraussetzungen,* 5 Lectures, Bern, 1924 (GA 309). **The Roots of Education** (Anthroposophic Press, 1996).

XX. *Der pädagogische Wert der Menschenerkenntnis und der Kulturwert der Pädagogik,* 10 Public Lectures, Arnheim, 1924 (GA 310). **Human Values in Education** (Rudolf Steiner Press, 1971).

XXI. *Die Kunst des Erziehens aus dem Erfassen der Menschenwesenheit,* 7 Lectures, Torquay, 1924 (GA 311). **The Kingdom of Childhood** (Anthroposophic Press, 1995).

XXII. *Geisteswissenschaftliche Impulse zur Entwicklung der Physik. Erster naturwissenschaftliche Kurs: Licht, Farbe, Ton—Masse, Elektrizität, Magnetismus,* 10 Lectures, Stuttgart, 1919–20 (GA 320). **The Light Course** (Steiner Schools Fellowship,1977).

XXIII. *Geisteswissenschaftliche Impulse zur Entwicklung der Physik. Zweiter naturwissenschaftliche Kurs: die Wärme auf der Grenze positiver und negativer Materialität,* 14 Lectures, Stuttgart, 1920 (GA 321). **The Warmth Course** (Mercury Press, 1988).

XXIV. *Das Verhältnis der verschiedenen naturwissenschaftlichen Gebiete zur Astronomie. Dritter naturwissenschaftliche Kurs: Himmelskunde in Beziehung zum Menschen und zur Menschenkunde,* 18 Lectures, Stuttgart, 1921 (GA 323). Available in typescript only as "**The Relation of the Diverse Branches of Natural Science to Astronomy**."

XXV. *The Education of the Child and Early Lectures on Education* (A collection) (Anthroposophic Press, 1996).

XXVI. Miscellaneous.

Index

DURING THE LAST TWO DECADES of the nineteenth century the Austrian-born Rudolf Steiner (1861–1925) became a respected and well-published scientific, literary, and philosophical scholar, particularly known for his work on Goethe's scientific writings. After the turn of the century he began to develop his earlier philosophical principles into an approach to methodical research of psychological and spiritual phenomena.

His multifaceted genius has led to innovative and holistic approaches in medicine, science, education (Waldorf schools), special education, philosophy, religion, economics, agriculture (Biodynamic method), architecture, drama, new arts of eurythmy and speech, and other fields. In 1924 he founded the General Anthroposophical Society, which today has branches throughout the world.

5648